Humor From the Bench

by

Donald N. Salvetti
Former Police Court Judge

Bloomington, IN   Milton Keynes, UK

AuthorHouse™
1663 Liberty Drive, Suite 200
Bloomington, IN 47403
www.authorhouse.com
Phone: 1-800-839-8640

AuthorHouse™ UK Ltd.
500 Avebury Boulevard
Central Milton Keynes, MK9 2BE
www.authorhouse.co.uk
Phone: 08001974150

This book is a work of non-fiction. Unless otherwise noted, the author and the publisher make no explicit guarantees as to the accuracy of the information contained in this book and in some

First published by AuthorHouse 7/19/2006

ISBN: 1-4259-4252-0 (sc)

Printed in the United States of America
Bloomington, Indiana

This book is printed on acid-free paper.

TABLE OF CONTENTS

PREFACE

This book is being authored by Donald N. Salvetti. He was elected Police Court Judge in the Village of Solvay, New York, on March 12, 1949. He served in that capacity for 12 years.

I think the title Police Court Judge was a little of a misnomer because his jurisdiction extended beyond police court matters and included all violations committed within the borders of his village: Traffic violations, juvenile violations, and criminal violations. His jurisdiction extended only, of course, to misdemeanors when it came to criminal matters. However, he did have original jurisdiction over all criminal matters, including murder. He had arraignment duties, and he also was able to hold preliminary hearings and then if he thought the case warranted further attention and further jurisdiction, he remanded the high-rate felony cases to the County Court. If he decided that his court found not a sufficient amount of evidence to warrant being remanded to the County Court, he would do so. But, the District Attorney's Office could submit all of the evidence to a Grand Jury and override the Police Court Judge's decision. Remember, in all felony cases, including murder, the Grand Jury must indict before a prosecution can take place. So it really didn't matter if the Police Court Judge decided there wasn't sufficient evidence, because the District Attorney could still submit the case to a Grand Jury.

I think I said that the Police Court Judge in the Village of Solvay had jurisdiction over all traffic violations. He had jurisdiction over juvenile court violations as long as he chose to do so. Otherwise, he remanded the cases involving juveniles to the Family Court Judge who sat in the court house in the city of Syracuse. The judge also had jurisdiction over civil matters, surprisingly, but the extent of the jurisdiction only permitted him to hear cases where the amount of money involved did not exceed $10,000. He also had jurisdiction over what we call Small Claims Court. This is a court in which the amount of money, or the relief sought, did not exceed $500. It was called small claims for that reason plus the fact that attorneys did not have to be present. In fact, the trials were conducted solely before the judge, which was myself, and he made the sole decision. Many of the rules of evidence were waived. So you can see that it was primarily a very informal venue.

As a matter of fact, one of the stories that I will be writing about in the second part of this book will be about a very interesting Small Claims Court case. The extent of the judges jurisdictional powers were more than I had anticipated, largely because the title of the office was Police Court Judge. However, I assumed my duties the day after election and proceeded to continue presiding over cases for 12 years.

I think you should know what the complexion of the Village of Solvay was. It was truly a cosmopolitan community. It was made up primarily of immigrants, when I was there when I became judge, and their children. The immigrants came from, it seemed, all parts of the world. Large segments of Italians, Austrians, Polish, Irish, Germans, Spanish, Portuguese, Swiss, made up for the most part 85 to 90 per cent of the population of Solvay. I think that these immigrants came to Solvay because of the great opportunity for work. The village contained several large manufacturing plants who I think came to Solvay because there was a large labor force and also because its employees didn't have to take a cab or ride a trolley car which was the only means of transportation to get to their work. They were all pretty much within walking distance from their place of employment. I could say truly it was a very cosmopolitan community. I could say truly that the people were very fiercely independent.

The City of Syracuse tried often, but failed, to annex the village to its boundaries. The people liked the government that they had made up of a mayor, six councilmen and their own judge. They liked the independence that they had as far as elections were concerned because they were able to elect their own representatives. They liked the fact that they could control their destiny. They had their own Police Department, their own Electrical Department, Water Department, Highway Department and etc. It was a very self-contained municipality, controlling all its functions. People liked being Solvaynians. They did not want to lose control of their government. Somehow they knew that if they became annexed to the City of Syracuse, their streets would be the last ones plowed, their schools would not be as well attended as they were or maintained, and they knew also that they would not know who their mayor was, nor who their councilman was as they did now. They liked their independence and you couldn't shake them from it. This was the community to which I was elected.

Mind you, a first generation Italian. I got my education at Syracuse University, both my Bachelors Degree at the University and my Law Degree at the Law School. As a matter of fact, it had always been my goal to become a lawyer and one day to run for office in my village and become its judge. That desire, that wish, that hope, reached reality in March of 1949. Becoming a judge and getting elected is not very easy.

Preparation

I had planned and worked hard for almost nine years, preparing myself for the day when I would run for that office. I joined all the clubs in the community, Kiwanas, Milton AC, Solvay Tigers AC, Young Business Communities; I was a member of Royal Order of Moose. I was also a member of Knights of Columbus, and the Junior Chamber of Commerce. I made sure that I became acquainted with, got known, and got myself liked by those people who eventually might vote for me. When I came back from service after World War II, I joined the two Veterans organizations that existed in my village, and in both instances I got elected Judge Post Advocate.

I wouldn't want to infer here that my election was fundamentally the result of the fact that I had joined so many clubs and organizations. That was not true. Of course, it helped but the main reason why I was elected was because the major portion, the largest number of voters in the village were either immigrants or children of immigrants and, of course, I was one of them.

I have found that in politics there is a certain affinity between immigrant groups. Polish candidates would certainly attract Polish voters. Italian candidates also attract Italian voters. Surprisingly, often enough, a Polish voter will even support an Italian candidate because he feels there is some kinship between himself and another person of foreign extraction. The fact that I was a first generation Italian really helped because my incumbent was not either a first generation citizen nor did he have any strong foreign attachments. I also have to say that one of the big reasons why I was elected in 1949 was because when we came back from the war in 1946, I learned and some of us Democrats learned that the Democratic Party was in total disarray and hadn't even put up a slate in the last two elections. Our village it seemed, as you might expect, was being operated as a one-party system, the Republican Party. That's never good and I knew that eventually the people of the village would not stand for it and they would probably, no doubt, give some support and help to the Democrats if we put up a slate which was worthy of their support

I recognized that I could not win the election as Police Court Judge solely on my own or if I ran solely on the ticket. I needed support, I needed to make sure that we had a whole slate, a mayor candidate and the three trustees, also candidates for the office.

As you might guess when one party is in complete control many things do not get done. In fact many complaints are ignored. This party, I recognized, felt that as long as they paid the bills, collected the taxes and reduced the debt they were doing what they were expected to do as officers conducting control of the Government. That was not satisfactory. The streets were full of potholes, the sidewalks and curbs had been washed away in many places, a whole tract called the Darrow Tract didn't have any storm sewers and when the rains were heavy there was a lot of damage done.

I checked the minutes at the village board of the village board meetings and found that a leader of this Darrow Tract appeared frequently at the board meetings and requested some action concerning the Darrow Tract because of the continued damage. He was told at each instance that they didn't have the money to spend to put in a storm system and that they were not going to borrow any more money to do it. That is, they wouldn't issue a bond issue and raise the money that way. They felt that the rest of the village didn't care what happened to the Darrow Tract. But that's not the way that you go.

I decided we had to reorganize the Democratic Party if we expected to win an election. So I took it upon myself to check the voters registration booklet and I sent a penny post card to every registered Democrat telling them what we planned to do and what was expected of them and hoped that they would come to the meeting that we had planned, give us some support, help us financially and also give us some suggestions as to how we could go about rebuilding our party and giving the Republican Party in our village some real honest-to-goodness opposition.

I sent out these cards and surprisingly they were well received. At the very first meeting we had well over 200 people who came to the meeting, listened to what was being said and seemed encouraged about the fact that we would be getting to see some life with reference to elections. We knew from the groups that appeared at these meetings we would have to select three trustee candidates, the mayor, and, of course, myself as a Police Court Judge candidate.

Our plans brought fruition. We met at the caucus date as provided by law, nominated a Mayor, Mr. Major, three trustees, and myself for Police Court Judge. Nobody in the village, or for that matter in the county, thought we had much of a chance of getting elected since we had very little staff, very little help, and certainly not very much money. However, we did our best. I raised some money which was to be used to hire workers. Each candidate paid for his own campaign cards which was only about $25 or $30 or so and I think we raised about $500 or so from fellow Democrats. So I would say that for the most part we only raised about $ 1,000 and that's how much we had to spend for this election.

I told you earlier I thought we had a chance to get elected. I was of the firm belief that the people of Solvay would not be content to sit by and watch their village be governed by one party to actually their detriment. We promised in the campaign that we'd do something about the potholes, we'd fix the walks, repair the curbs, resurface Milton Avenue where the old Trolley Car rails were still intact and in fact in some places even protruded up over and above the pavement. You can imagine what danger that brought about. We also promised that we would do something about a program. We promised that we would float a bond issue and install storm sewers in the Darrow Tract. Well, we won the election to the surprise of not only those whom we defeated but both newspapers were sharply surprised that we had turned out the Republicans in our village. I got elected judge, the mayor got elected and we elected two trustees. Not enough to completely control the village but enough to make a big stand. The very next year we elected two more trustees and then took control of the village and went on to accomplish what we had promised the people we would if elected and placed in control.

Believe me we did what we promised the people we would do. We floated the bond issue, installed storm sewers in the Darrow Tract, we repaired all the potholes, we repaired the walks and curbs, we resurfaced Milton

Avenue and removed the danger there. We also started a parks program. One, even a small park in every section of the village so that the kids, the little kids, could enjoy some activity in the park. We installed swings, kiddy cars and so forth. We actually increased the summer park force by at least ten or fifteen people. Each little park had a director, programs were promulgated and these directors did a remarkable job of running and controlling the little parks.

I mentioned also, I think, that we had promised the village people that we would furnish them with a bath house and a swimming pool which was so terribly needed, especially if you were going to have a summer program where the kids could stay out of trouble, enjoy themselves and have fun. We floated a bond issue which was only for $250,000. That bond issue made it possible for us to build a bath house, swimming pool, a Softball park. We had a baseball park on Woods Road. That's where the hard ball was played but the Softball games used the Softball park that we built with that money we raised with the bond issue and developed a large park/playground facility for the people of Solvay. This was a remarkable event.

I want to make it clear that it was not only because of the number of clubs and organizations I had joined all those years in preparation for this office, but that there were other factors involved and I think one of the primary factors, making it possible for me to win the election, was that so many of the people in the village were either immigrants or children of immigrants. As I said earlier, the community was made up primarily of European Countries. We had people here who came from Italy, Spain, Portugal, Austria, France, Switzerland, Poland, Ireland, Russia and, of course, as I mentioned we had Afro-American families. I think this was largely due to the fact that so many immigrants and their progeny felt they had to support fellow immigrants, which I was. I think there is a little bit of affinity between people of foreign extraction. I think many of the people I contacted in Solvay were of foreign extraction.

I remember when I was back in school, and I graduated from Solvay High School in 1932, almost all of us kids in the classroom were sons and daughters of immigrants. Well, that was pretty much what the nature of the village was at the time.

We needed more than just some help from these National groups. We needed to have a party that people could support, help, and assist in overcoming the dominance that was evident in Solvay back in 1949.

When I came home from service, I noticed that the Democratic Party was in disarray and that the Republican Party in our village didn't have any opposition in the last two elections, hi fact, our village when I got home from service, was being governed by a one-party system. I think this was a feature that helped us get elected in 1949. I remember going over the village board minutes and finding very often that complaints, requests, demands, and general acts of hope from the board, fell on deaf ears. I remember particularly a representative being up there who came from the Darrow Tract This fellow, I mink, appeared almost at every board meeting, and he kept requesting that the village somehow, some way install storm sewers in their area, because when the rains came down heavily it did considerable damage to all their property. You see, the whole tract was built on the side hill, and the rain when it poured, gushed down and did damage to their lawns and their driveways. I have to believe that this arrogance, independence, and lack of concern on the part of the village power men helped us immeasurably when we ran against them in 1949.

The condition of the village was in poor shape. There were potholes in the highways, there were a number of sidewalks and curbs missing, damaged by ice falls, heavy floods, the main street in Solvay had the old trolley tracks sticking out there. In many instances, some of the old rails from the trolley tracks still stuck out from the pavement. These, of course, were very dangerous to the few cars that were in operation at the time. I think that all these factors helped us win.

I do want to point out that I took it upon myself to check all the names of the registered Democrats in the registration book. What I did was send them all a penny postcard, telling them what we planned to do and asking them to come to a meeting where we would discuss the possibilities of running a slate, perhaps some of them would even run for office, but at least we would get their views, suggestions and ideas. We made it clear to all these Democrats who appeared at these meetings- we had several of them--that we were going to run a Democratic slate come March of 1949. The Republicans were no longer going to win by default.

At the time of the caucus, we were prepared to nominate a slate, which we did. We nominated a mayor, three trustees and myself. I pretty much put into place this effort, because I knew that if I were to run for Police Court Judge in my village, I needed more than just myself on the ticket. We had to have a full slate and we managed to do so. We appeared, nominated our candidates and ran in the election; didn't have much money. I put up most of the money, but we did raise about $500 from the Democrats in the village, plus what I had contributed, we had close to $1,000 to use for election purposes.

The candidates, paid for their own campaign cards. That is the extent of their contribution. I guess they didn't want to spend much money because primarily they thought they didn't have much of a chance of winning anyway. So, why spend a lot of money which they feared would be wasted. Well, it wasn't wasted. We were elected by close margins but elected, nevertheless. We did not take control of the village because we only elected two trustees and, of course, there are six on the board. But the next year we won two out of three that ran for trustee and we took control of the village government and then we began to do the things we promised the people we would if elected in 1949.

Our next big project was to provide what we promised: A swimming pool, a bath house and a large playground facility for the people of Solvay. We floated a bond issue for $250,000 and used that money to do what we said we would. We built a bath house, a swimming pool, and provided a large play ground for all the kids in Solvay who attended very faithfully all summer long. We did what we said we would do and surprisingly enough, we never raised the tax rate one penny. We did it by eliminating all the foolishness, unwise spending, and the favoritism that had been shown by the party originally involved.

Beginning to Serve

I had reviewed for you pretty much the condition of our village at the time we were elected to office-- particularly when I was elected to office. I had served twelve years and then did not choose to run for a fourth term because for a large part, I had to go out and make more money, because I had four kids who were going to need my financial support when they got ready to go to college. Now, that is pretty much how we stood back in 1949 when I took office.

Unexpected Service

I would now like to tell you about the things that happened, the experiences I encountered, most of which I didn't expect before I ran for office. I didn't know, or didn't expect, or hadn't thought that I would be called upon frequently to marry people.

Wedding

It so turned out that I was called upon by many couples to marry them. Being Catholic myself, I really thought that people would be getting married by a priest or a minister or some member who headed their church. I didn't think I would be called upon as often as I was, being a lay person, but I was. I did it and I wasn't reluctant. I knew it was part of my civic duty, and I carried it out.

I do want to report one particular wedding ceremony that I performed that stuck for along time in my memory. The bride had called upon me to marry her and her fiancee. I thought it would be just a normal, brief, quick experience, as in the past, but I wasn't told. She wanted to know if I could be at her home about 2:00 o'clock in the afternoon on a given Saturday. I told her I was pretty sure I could do so.

When I got to the house, I was ushered into the parlor which was loaded with people and beautifully decorated and I was walked over to a makeshift alter also well decorated with flowers and candles. I stood there at the alter for a few moments and listened to the piano player who very softly played "Here Comes the Bride." And soon, down the open staircase, into the parlor came the bride all dressed in white, white veil and all, preceded by her bridesmaid, and marching down the stairs on the arm of her father who, as it turned out, was to give her away. He walked her over to the alter and stepped back to be with his wife.

The groom and his best man were over by the alter to my left and the bride walked over accompanied by her bridesmaid of honor, to my right. I knew that this was not going to be any ordinary, simple marriage ceremony, so I dug down deep into my memory box to see if I could come up with something very appropriate to the occasion. So, I began "Dearly beloved we are gathered here to witness the union of this lovely bride and her fiancee Bob Jones." (Name fictitious) I turned to the two and said, "Please repeat after me. Dearly beloved, I wish thee to be my lawful wedded wife to hold and to have her all my life." I asked Mary (name fictitious) to repeat the same thing after me. Once this had been done, I asked the best man to give the ring to the groom and the maid of honor to give her ring to the bride. I turned to the groom and said, "I want you to repeat after me while you put this ring on Mary's third finger of her left hand", which he did, and he repeated after me the following words: "With this ring I thee wed and I want it to be a symbol of my love for you forever." I turned to Mary and told her I wanted her to do the same thing, she placed the ring on the third finger of his left hand and repeated after me: "With this ring, I thee wed, and it is also a symbol of my everlasting love for you." I said to the bride and groom, "Please hold hands," and I said after they did that, "Now in the presence of all these people by the power invested in me by the State of New York I hereby pronounce thee man and wife, you may kiss the bride. God bless this union and all your friends here who are witness to this union."

Speechmaking

Another experience which I didn't anticipate before I was elected, was the number of times I was called upon to make speeches. You see, I had been the only Democrat in upstate New York elected judge, and, of course, I was the only Italian/American who had been elected judge in all of Central New York. So, you can see why I was called upon frequently by many Democratic organizations to appear and be the principal speaker. I didn't believe there were as many Italian organizations as I learned there were after I became Police Court Judge. I was called upon frequently to be present, make the principal speech, at all their installation dinners. I remember my wife keeping count of the number of nights I had gone out from the house to appear at these various occasions. She totaled up the number of nights I was away from home, I believe it was the Month of March or April, out of the 30 days or 31 days of the month, I was out 21 days. So, you can see, I was kept pretty busy--but, I enjoyed it.

I liked the fact that I met so many people. I was especially pleased to be called upon by the Democrats to tell them how we had succeeded in overturning the Republican Party in our village, and I especially enjoyed talking to the Italian Clubs, because, after all, I felt a strong kinship to all those people, particularly thinking that most of them had voted for me when I was elected. Of course, I had some pride in the fact that I was the only Italian/American judge in the whole Central New York area.

Youth Counseling

Another experience that occurred to me was the number of parents that called upon me to "talk" to their children primarily about matters of sex. Well, I was no expert of course, but I do recall that when I was at Syracuse University, we all had to take as a compulsory course, boys and girls in our freshman year a course in hygiene. It was primarily a course in sex education. I do remember--it's funny that I can recall after all this time--my professor at the time was a Dr. Hickerno. And, I think I remember him because one of his favorite expressions was. "Boys, I want to tell you, girls do not get pregnant by riding a bicycle in a high wind. You know how they get pregnant, so behave yourself, take care of yourself and stay out of trouble."

Of course, the lectures were more than that. I used that same statement to the boys when I was asked to talk to them about sex. But when I talked to the girls primarily, I warned them about the various promises or statements the boys would make when making love to them. I told them not to believe the boys who tell them they can't get pregnant unless they have an orgasm. That's a lot of bunk. Some boys tell the girls that they can't get pregnant if they have sex while they're menustrating. That's more bunk. "I want to tell you girls," I used to say to them, "There's only one real way for you to keep from getting pregnant, and that is to avoid having any sexual contact." They'll promise you anything--they'll promise you that they'll marry you and they'll also say that if you're not good to them and succumb to their wishes, they won't call upon you any more or they won't be your boyfriend. It's not worth it. Please, believe me.

I used to tell the boys when I had them alone in a session, pretty much the same thing. Don't be promising these girls all those things that you think you can do. Believe me, and you may not realize it, if you get this girl pregnant, and she's under 16 years of age that's great proof, real proof, that you have committed second degree rape and if her parents want to pursue it, you can be in real trouble legally. I don't know why it's important for you to have sex. Please, this can only bring trouble.

Remember, if you are the father of a child born out of wedlock, you can be made to support that child until that child is 18 years of age. Just imagine yourself working struggling, trying to get ahead and having to support a child until he or she is 18 years of age.

I want to tell you also, don't depend upon condoms, they too can be unsuccessful. The best bet and the one that my mother always gave me when admonishing me in matters of this kind was to keep your penis in your pocket.

I don't know whether all these speeches that I gave to these kids helped any or not. You know, you do your best, you tell them what you think is best for them and you go on from there.

Philanthropic Fund Raising

There were other experiences that I encountered after being elected judge that I like to talk about. I found that because I held a prominent position in the village, I was called upon frequently to head up the drive for Boys Town, Community Chest, Help the Flood Victims in Italy, March of Dimes, Salvation Army--you name it. I didn't mind heading up these drives because they're all for worthy causes. I didn't mind doing my part for these worthy causes. But I want to tell you, they take a lot of time. Heading up these drives isn't something that you can do in an hour or two a day or an hour or two here and there. They take a lot of time, a lot of phone calls, a lot of personal time, a lot of management time organizing crews, getting other people to help you. It's very, very demanding But I did it knowing that it was expected of me and besides, I felt that was a service that I should have expected when I was elected.

Another experience that I witnessed after I got elected Police Court Judge was more of a personal nature. You see, I could no longer go into a public tavern and drink beer or something stronger with the boys because somehow it didn't look right but on one occasion especially a couple of drunks brought up before me in court looked me in the eye and said, "Hey Judge didn't we have a great time last night down at Duffel's Tavern." I didn't like that and I knew I had to do something about it, so I just stopped going into taverns where I might meet up with the same possible situation.

Another thing that I had to be careful about was who rode in my car. Who would be seen riding with me. If it were some good-looking young blonde, I was sure that in no time at all the gossipers would be pedalng around the village that I was carrying on with some young girl. Anything to make me look bad. So, many is the time I would drive by the bus stop and not pick up the girl who was going in the same direction as I was, maybe to the courthouse. I couldn't risk it.

I also found--let me say first, that generally at the Milton A Cs Club that I belonged to, we met once a month, and after the meeting was over, we'd gather around the table to play a little poker until 12:00 o'clock. I enjoyed those poker games. We didn't gamble for much--it was a nickels and dimes game, but it was fun and I enjoyed it. But I thought, after I was elected judge, "What if there was a raid, what if the police came in and found me there playing poker with the boys." I wasn't sure whether this club had an exemption or not. It was a private club but we were not maintaining really private quarters. We were holding the meetings in some vacant building. So, because there was some doubt as to whether or not this little bit of gambling that went on was not illegal, I couldn't take the chance-I couldn't take the risk. So, I forsake that little pleasure that I enjoyed.

You see, being the judge in a village. You're under exposure of all kinds. You had to be careful. How are you dressed? How do you conduct yourself? How you speak? How you act toward people. And, in many instances, you're subject to a great many restraints you've never had to endure before. But, that's the price you pay when you run for office and get elected.

Youthful Judge

I must say that on three occasions after I was elected to office, my youth came into play. I have always been taken to be younger than I really am, and it is so today. Anyway, I was sitting up on the bench going over some papers when this nice little old lady came in walked over to the bench and asked me if she could see the judge. I thought for a moment that she was pulling my leg but I noticed that she was sincere so I said, "Well, if you'll just wait a little while, the judge will be here shortly and you can discuss with him your problem. Won't you please walk over there and sit down in the court room? He'll be with you shortly." Right after that, the courtroom began to fill up with those who had received tickets and summonses to appear in my court.

I presided over the cases and finally dispensed with all the ones that were before me. Then I turned to the lady who was sitting there almost by herself in the courtroom and asked her to come forward. She did. I said, "Tell me Ma'am, what's your problem?" She stood there and looked at me for almost a full minute and said, "Why didn't you tell me that you were the judge?" I was at a loss for words, but managed to say, "Well really, Ma'am, I thought you were kidding me." She said, "Oh, I wasn't kidding you, I really have a problem, but I think you're too young to be a judge-at least I thought so at the time. That's why I didn't recognize you. But, after I saw you preside over the cases that were before you here this morning, I changed my mind. I don't think age has anything to do with it, I found you to be very competent, I thought you handled yourself very well, and I'm really happy to bring to you my problem which is my neighbor next door.

"I like to go to sleep about 11:00 o'clock at night and my bedroom is on the side of the house that faces his house. He plays the radio very loud, even after 11:00 o'clock at night. I think even the people down the street can hear it. I've told him about it, but he ignores my complaint. I talked to the judge who was here before you and he told me I should sue him. Well, I don't want to go that far. I thought maybe you being a new judge you might have some different ideas." I said, "Ma'am, I think I can help you. Go downstairs and walk into the police room and talk to the sergeant on duty. Tell him that I sent you down there and that you are to give him the name and address of the man who lives next door as well as your own. I'll be down there shortly and see what I can do.

A few minutes later I went down and asked the lady if she had a ride home, she said, No." I said, "OK, stand by and we'll take care of you." I told the sergeant at the desk to call for one of the patrolmen to take her home and I also told the sergeant to tell the patrolman to give this message to the man next door. He was to tell him that he has no business playing that radio as loudly as he does after 11:00 o'clock at night. And tell him the judge said he must turn that radio off at 11:00 o'clock at night so people can go to sleep or turn it down so softly that he's the only one who could hear it. I said to the policeman, "You tell that fellow that if he doesn't do this, I'm going to swear out a warrant against him for disorderly conduct." I turned to lady and said, "I think that will do it." She thanked me, and off she went.

Another Youthful Judge Incident

The next case in which my youth came into play, was the time when I had been called upon to give a speech at one of those clubs. They were installing new officers for the year. I had told the president of the club that I would be little late because I had a prior engagement but not to fear, I would be there to make the speech.

I wasn't quite as late as I thought I would be and got there just in time to sit down and enjoy the dinner. There were a couple of vacant chairs at the head table and I took one and sat next to this very young, attractive lady. We had some conversation--not much and I noticed that she kept looking at the door, looking at the door, and seemed to get more anxious every time she looked at the door. Finally, I said, "What's the problem Ma'am. You seem to be watching that door very closely and you don't seem very calm." She said, "Our main speaker is a judge, Judge Salvetti, who is supposed to come here and speak to us and I know he told the president he would be a little late so I'm worried, I'm really afraid that he may not show up in time to make the speech. If he doesn't get here pretty soon, the installation of the officers will be over and that's pretty much what will happen here." I looked her in the eye and thought, "Could it be possible that this young lady doesn't know that I'm the Judge and I'm going to give the principal speech." But, apparently she didn't because she kept looking at the door and saying almost to herself, "My God, it's getting late, it's getting late."

At any rate, the President finished with his small, brief remarks, then turned to me, put his hand on my shoulder and said, "Now the toastmistress will introduce you with a little, small biographical sketch, our speaker of the evening, Judge Salvetti." He turned to the toastmistress and said, "Take over, Ma'am, and introduce the judge." Well, you could have hit her with a sledge hammer. She looked at me--really gave me a dirty look. She got up, introduced me by telling the people a little something about how I happened to get elected, a little something about my background, and also a little something about my achievements as judge.

I gave my speech--I think it was well received. At least the applause indicated as much, and sat down. The toastmistress turned to me and said, "Why are you doing this to me?" Again I wasn't sure how to answer. I said, "Ma'am, I thought you were pulling my leg. Didn't you know that I was the Judge? Didn't you know that I got elected a few months ago and I thought probably you were just kidding me?" She said, "No such thing, you fooled me, and I didn't like it." And then I said, "What made you think that the person who sat next to you at the head table was not the person who was going to be making the speech and who was the judge?" She said, "To be honest with you, I didn't think you were the judge, because you looked too young to be the judge." We had a few words, I apologized, and completed the function. Again, it seems that my age was something that interfered with people determining who I was.

Conduct Complaint

Another occasion, much later, the state trooper who was attached to the BCI, which is the Criminal Investigation Arm of the State Police, asked to see me. He was ushered into my office, sat down and showed me a letter he had gotten from the governor. He said, "The Governor had a complaint about your conduct. As was the custom, he just turned the complaint over to me and told me to investigate it, so here I am." I looked the trooper in the eye and said, "Complaint about my conduct. Well, that's something I wasn't aware of. I really don't believe I've done anything wrong." The State Trooper said, "Well, I kind of believe the same thing. What she complained about was that in a trial about two week ago, you practically told the jury to acquit the defendant." "I told the jury to acquit a defendant. I don't know why I would do that," I said. The trooper went on. He said, "She said you told the jury they had to acquit or convict the defendant by a unanimous vote and you also told the jury that the decision as to whether or not he was guilty has to be beyond a reasonable doubt. She went on to explain to the governor that practically meant that the jury was to find the defendant not guilty."

"It's apparent and evident that she didn't know the law. It was my duty to tell the jury that they could not convict this defendant unless they did so beyond a reasonable doubt. That's the law and I followed it." The trooper said, "I was sure, Judge, that you wouldn't be making any serious mistake of a sufficient nature for the Governor to take action as severe as removing you from office. I'll report to the governor that the complaint that you had instructed the jury to find the defendant not guilty was unfounded. And, also, I forgot to mention she said that you were too young to be a judge, and you could not know enough about judging to be sitting on the bench and ought to be removed." I kind of chuckled about that because this was the second time that my youth came into play. People just didn't think I was as old as I was. I was 37 years old at the time and certainly old enough to take over the duties of a Police Court Judge.

There were other occasions when the people felt that I was too young to be a judge but, in time, I convinced them. The ability, as far as judging was concerned, was much more important than youth.

PTA Meetings

I told you earlier that I was very often called upon to talk to certain groups and to parents and to people who were interested in learning a little more about the things, primarily legal, that affected their lives.

On one occasion I remember being called upon to speak at a PTA Meeting about juvenile delinquency. After talking at length about some of the problems involved, I told the group, "I leave you with a couple of thoughts. One is, if you can't tell your child what to do, how to behave, or how to accept discipline, when he's six, you certainly won't be able to tell him what to do, how to accept discipline, or how to behave when he or she is sixteen."

I also told the group that very often people will tell them, "You've got to let the children have their own way frequently for the most part because that's how they learn. That's how they learn to behave properly, that's how they learn to live a decent life." I said to the group, "Don't pay any attention to those kinds of stories, or injunctions, remember you are the parent. Let's say for example that you're standing on a pier, and your daughter is standing right there next to you. You look down in the water and there are sharks swimming around close by. Your daughter wants to dive into the water and do some swimming. I ask, should you let her do so, or should you do everything you can to prevent her doing so? That's what I mean about allowing children to do so much on their own and to go just so far. You are the parent, you must exercise certain disciplines and you must make sure that you protect them by your actions from doing things at their age that may result in disaster."

Political and Ethnic Group Speeches

I also told you earlier that I was called upon frequently to make speeches to especially Democratic groups and Italian/American groups. I must tell you about this one occasion in which I was called upon to make this principal speech-it was a BIG occasion--almost 400 people had bought tickets to the dinner. The dinner and the party was to take place in the Main Ballroom of the Hotel Syracuse.

I was told by the President of the organization called "Voters of Italian Extraction" to make sure that I gave a speech that would be long remembered. This would be the largest group before whom I would address any remarks. This would also be a very critical group, because it would be made up of supposedly voters of Italian extraction. The president of the association told me he expected that I would make some remarks about politics because these were supposedly people who voted and supposedly would be interested in learning more about what their duty should be or how they should go about functioning and working to make sure that their kind were placed into office. I assured the president that I would make a few remarks about politics but that would not be the main theme of my speech. I said, "I'm saving what I have to say in that speech for an occasion such as this--a large group of Italian people who have come to hear and listen to a speech by one of their own kind."

I was also a voter of Italian extraction. I never called myself a voter of Italian extraction or never said I was of Italian extraction or Italian/American. I said I was Italian. Irish always said they were Irish, even though they were born here in America of Irish parents, the same for the Jewish people, the same for the Germans, the same for the English, same for the Spanish. It seemed that they all called themselves either Irish, German, English, French, Spanish, Polish. But when it came to Italians, it seemed proper to be called Italian/American. We are Americans. We were born here in America-whether you're black, yellow, brown--born of any foreign people, Chinese, Japanese--if you're born here in America, you're an American. I considered myself an

American; but, I also considered myself to be an Italian because my parents were both Italian and I was proud of the fact that I belonged to a very special ethnic group. At any rate, I told the president that I would be making a speech that night that I hoped they would remember and I hoped they would accept gracefully.

The night of the dinner arrived, I was up there on the platform at the dais, certain speeches were being made by different officers of the organization and then the toastmaster called upon me. The ballroom was just completely full of people. Whoever planned this affair certainly did a good job. At any rate, I knew I had my work cut out for me so I proceeded as follows: I said, "Hello, Italians and those who wish they were. I bring you greetings. I do not come here to tell you what you should do politically to advance our cause. I do not plan to tell you, because I think you already know that you must stand together, support one another, and give aid and assistance to one another if one of your number happens to be on the ticket. I do not propose to tell you because I think you already know that success in the election is only possible if the person running that you hope to elect gets financial aid; so please, consider all those elements and do your best to make sure that in the future we will be represented in all phases of government through our own elective efforts and as a result receive the true benefits that we are entitled to as Americans, that Government has to offer.

"But my main purpose in speaking to you tonight is not going to be about politics. It's going to be about us, 'We'. We have unquestionably a mighty powerful heritage. People of our nationality have succeeded in the past in every phase of endeavor, be it music - Verdi, Donnatelli; be it science--Enrico Fermi, who it is said, was the father of the atomic bomb, Galileo, Marconi, Leonardi DaVinci, said to be the greatest genius of all time, Toscanini and, of course, the man who discovered America, Christopher Columbus; and, remember too that these Italians reached great heights and we should be very proud of that heritage. Remember too, that even these two continents, North and South America received their name from Americus Vespuci an Italian explorer who explored the two continents and wrote about them and the continents were subsequently named America after Americus Vespuci. "Cabot Guillermo Corbati. was also a famous explorer, history tells us who did much to tell the world about the new continents. I think I left out Rafael, Michalangelo, Dante--but at any rate most of us here know who these great men were and why we should feel so proud that we also are the product of this great National ethnicity.

"I also want to point out that those of us who are a first generation of Italian immigrants have done pretty well here in America. We have excelled in sports, we've excelled in music, we've excelled in teaching, we've excelled in law, we've excelled in medicine. In every phase of American life we have taken prime, top-notch positions. You know who they are: DiMaggio, Bera, Marciano, Sarazen. In the field of banking-Gioni, manufacturing--Joseph Petrifaci. We also have from our own National Group produced people like Mario Cuomo, Charles Paleti. It would seem if one were to make a full study of the various conditions and the history of the last two or three centuries it would find that those of us of Italian extraction, that is those of us who have inherited from our people our heritage, stand out here in America in one generation extremely successful.

Immigrant Grandparents and Parents

"I one time asked my grandfather how it was that we had an Italian, Christopher Columbus, discover America but then it took us about 400 years later to come here. The English came here before us, the Irish, the Dutch, Germans, Scandinavians, Swedes. We were about the last group of all. He looked at me and said, 'Son, it's not such a bad thing! When we came here, the roads had already been built, the bridges were in place, factories had been installed, land had been cleared away, schools had been built, hospitals were built, governmental buildings were built, we didn't have to fight the Indians; so, believe me, we weren't so dumb after all.' I had never quite thought of it that way. But then I said. 'Grandpa, why did you decide to come to America?' Then he said, 'Son, in my town I used to hear the people talk about America being a place where gold was in the streets. I thought I had better go over there and pick some of that up before it's all gone. So, I saved my money, which was pretty hard because we were paid so little for our work. But at any rate, I made it to America.

'When I got off the boat and when I left Ellis Island, I went up to the first policeman and I said, 'Tell me, where shall I go to find this gold that's in the street?' And he looked at me and he said, 'You see that sign down there that says 'Men Wanted'? Go down there and they'll take care of you.' So, I rushed over to the place, talked to the man in charge. He said, 'Yes, we've been looking for people like you.' He handed me a pick and shovel. 'You go out and see that man out there, he's the foreman of that job. You start digging with that pick and shovel and you'll find your gold.' My grandfather went out to the boss man. The boss man knew why he was there, and the boss man set him to digging the ditch. After my grandfather had dug three or four feet, he turned to the boss and said, 'You know, I haven't found any gold. I thought the gold was lying out here in the street.' The boss said, 'No, you're misinformed, you have to dig for it..' 'Oh, I see.' He said, 'Oh, and by the way, you didn't go down deep enough. You gotta go down another two feet. You gotta dig down about two feet more, six feet in total. Perhaps then you'll begin to find the gold. But, remember, it isn't just lying there. You've gotta look for it. And, it isn't every two feet you're going to find a pile of gold. There just isn't that much there, so just keep right on digging.' My grandfather told me that he and the rest of them who came here with the idea of finding gold on the street, found themselves digging six-foot ditches all along the highways in New York City which, he said, became the sewer lines and the water lines of the city. And there was no gold.

"He said he caught on quite quickly, sent a letter to his brother-in-law and told his brother-in-law he wished to come there to live. The brother-in-law wrote back, he said, and told him, 'You're welcome, jobs up here are very plentiful, and I think you'll make out.' That was my grandfather's story.

"My father didn't come here looking for gold. He was sixteen years old when he came here to America. It was here in America that he met his wife and married her, my mother. She was born here, first born of my grandfather Peacher. At any rate, my father said he came here for the purpose of raising enough money to give him a stake that he could use when he went back to Italy to buy a farm or to buy a business, because his father who had a silk business would have to, under the laws of Italy, leave it entirely to the first-born son. You see, in Italy, in those days, the law of Primogeniture was in effect. The first-born son got the property and this was done so that the property wouldn't be divided up into so many small parcels and so small that nobody who got the inheritance would be able to survive. But I have to say, I'm very happy that my father came here to America for the purpose of raising enough money to go back and live the good life. He liked it here, he liked the freedom, he liked the opportunities, he liked the opportunities that were afforded a family and he liked the people who were, he said, pretty much in the same boat. Most of them immigrants, maybe from different countries, but at least they were immigrants. And he said he liked the fact that the people made the decisions as to who would rule over them. This was not so in Italy or for that matter in practically any European country.

Scholarships for Education

After telling that story about my father, I turned to the subject which is dearest to my heart. I told the audience that somewhere out there was another Enrico Caruso, another Enrico Fermi, another Toscanini, another Leonardo DaVinci, another Michalangelo, another Dante or Galileo and that they could not further their education because they lacked the funds. They could not become what we'd like to see them become in America. The opportunity was there but the money and the financial aid was missing. "So, my friends, I'm telling you tonight that what we need here in America so that those 'would be' youngsters can achieve their goals, is an Italian Education Trust Fund.. We must raise thousands of dollars and make it possible for those who have the talent and who are worthy of the help to pursue their ambition; and, when we do that, we will have accomplished our goal and our objective which is to continue not to lean heavily upon the past celebrities who have become famous in history--but we will be able to see our own first generation, second generation, third generation Italians become famous and worthy of great American admiration.

"I am sick and tired of picking up a newspaper and reading for the most part about bosses, gangsters, and Mafia. I want to pick up the paper and read about Johnny and Mary and other Italians like them who have achieved greatness because they had the opportunity and took advantage of it. So, let us begin tonight to start this foundation and raise the money and make it possible for our kind to achieve greatness. I have here in my hand a check for $100 made payable to the Italian Scholarship Foundation. I hope that many of you in this room will follow suit. We can raise enough money right here in this room to proudly give advanced educational opportunities to a great many children of our nationality. Let us begin!. Thank you for coming and God bless you all. Remember to drive safely because the life you save may be mine."

I do say the applause was thunderous. I guess my speech was well received. I know that the people who heard me won't forget what I said and I know too, that somehow they will take to heart my suggestion that we raise the funds to make it possible for these coming youngsters, growing youngsters here in our country of Italian extraction will have an opportunity from us for which we will be proud.

I made other speeches to other groups and in many instances I leaned heavily upon the people who came before us and whom we thought were so successful in history--the Galileos, the Fermis, Toscaninis, and so forth; but, I don't think I made a speech that was as strong as the one I made when I spoke to the Voters of Italian Extraction. At any rate, I thought someone had to talk about and explain to people in his speeches why we have become so proud and that we can continue to do the things to make the coming generations also proud. I thought I was doing my duty by pointing out to the people that we couldn't just sit back and rest on the laurels of all those great people who came before us. We had responsible for producing new heroes, new leaders, new scientists, new musicians, and new people for whom we could be very proud.

Election Issues

One in particular that amused me was one that had to do with the reelection of a County Judge. My party chairman came to me and said, "Judge, how would you like to run for county judge? The Governor appointed Albert Orhnstein to fill a vacancy that occurred because one of the judges retired. We need a candidate. You always win in your bailiwick so maybe you might do the same here so we'd like to nominate you. I said, "Sure, I've got nothing to lose." So, I undertook to run for the office.

In the past whenever I had run for any office--I ran for family court once before and nearly got elected. Thank God I didn't because all I'd be doing there would be presiding over cases involving child support and juvenile cases that are insoluble. You don't know what to do with kids that get into trouble. At any rate, I made up my mind that if I were to have any chance of winning

Donald N. Salvetti

I should have to go to the outer areas, what we call the "sticks" towns that were way out beyond the city line that were maybe nine to one Republican. I thought if I had a chance to win on this occasion I had to convince a few people in these outer towns. So I would call a few of the Democratic Women and arrange for a political supper. In other words, the Democrat Women would get other Democrat Women to bring covered dishes to a supper. I would furnish the ham and the roast beef. In that way I thought I would make a few friends and get a few extra votes and possibly win the election.

On this one occasion I recall, everything went off beautifully. We had our supper and I was called upon by this Committeewoman who was a Democrat to give my little speech and explain to the people who were there why I thought they should vote for me. Well, I discussed a number of things that I thought would be of interest like Capital Punishment, Juvenile Delinquency Crime, Plea Bargaining, and so forth. I thought I had made a pretty good presentation. Then, of course, you usually ask if there are any questions. So, I asked the group if there were any questions they would like to ask of me, I would like to accommodate them if I could. Well, a lady in the front row raised her hand and said, "May I ask a question, Judge?" I said, "Sure, go right ahead." She said, "Albert Orinstein is running for County Court

Judge on the Republican Ticket and you, Don Salvetti, are running for County Court Judge on the Democratic Ticket?" I said, "Yes, that's so." She said, "Well, tell me, are there any American's running for this office?" Well, I paused for a moment and I said, "Yes, Ma 'am, there are. Albert Orenstein is an American, I'm an American and there is a fellow running on the American Labor Party Ticket by the name of O'Hara. That's about it. The three of us running for office are all Americans."

I thought afterward this "dyed-in-the-wool" Republican from this town where there were more cows than there were people--I could imagine she voting for a member of the American Labor Party. But at any rate, that's one of the experiences I had that I'll never forget and really I got a big kick out of it.

Paycheck Dilemma

I don't think people know this but, at any rate, I undertook to do something about it and that was: often the poor women had to try to get along with very little money. It was embarrassing-embarrassing to me, the judge, and I think embarrassing to the people in authority.

It would seem that on occasion the husband of these women would stop at a beer joint on the way home and practically spend half of his pay before he got home. Then he turned over the balance of his paycheck to his wife and of course she couldn't make ends meet with half the pay and she didn't know where to turn so she came to me for help. That is this particular case; I've had several, but this particular one came to me for help. Most of the time I'd tell them to take the matter up with the Family Court Judge. The Family Court Judge would probably do something about it. But in this case he brought such a little amount of money home that she practically had nothing to buy food with. I thought I had better step in and see what I could do so I called the husband in and I got the story pretty much the same. He said, "Well," he said, "I don't know, I cashed my paycheck, I stopped in at the saloon, I got to drinking. Somebody bought me a drink and I bought them a drink. The next thing I know", he said, "half of my pay check was gone. I told my wife I was sorry and I gave her all I had." She said, "How am I supposed to run this house with just half a pay check?" So, she said, "I think maybe we had better talk to the judge because he may be able to do something." So, I said, "Mr. Jones (name fictitious) it's pretty hard for you to leave the plant in the company of some other men and stop in the saloon, have a few drinks." He said, "Yes, your honor, I really feel embarrassed when they say 'come on along' and I say 'I can't, I gotta go straight home'--it makes it pretty difficult." I said, "I'll tell you what we're gooing to do. Ma 'am you're goong to meet your husband at the gate when he gets out of work and you're going to accompany him over to Reboza's Tavern. He's going to cash his check there because I understand she cashes the checks for the men working at the Solvay Processing Company. When he cashes the check he is to give you all of the money except $5. I suggest that he keep the $5 out of his paycheck, which is not much but at least it's a little, and probably you can't afford it either but he works hard all week. I think he ought to have a little money, a little something, so he can buy a drink or two, maybe go bowling, or at least have a few bucks in his pocket. I hope you agree to that." She said, "Yes, I understand. He's gotta have a little money. After all he does work hard all week and", she said, "to tell you the truth Judge he's a good husband, he's good to the kids, good to me. But every once in a while he comes home and gives me only half the pay. I just can't make it go, I can't make a go of it. Okay, we'll try to do what you say." So, I said, "Is that okay with you Mr. Jones?" He said, "Yes." I said, "Alright now, don't feel embarrassed, don't feel upset. You can go off to the corner somewhere, avoid the other men who might be coming out of work with you. Take your wife in, buy her a beer when you get one for yourself. Make it appear as though she just met you to have a beer. Then when you get through be sure you take $5 for yourself and give the rest of the money to her. I hope this solves the problem." They thanked me and off they went.

I had a number of cases such as that but not too many, just enough. It seemed to work out. I was glad that I was able to work out some kind of solution and keep harmony in the family. I figured that's part of my job. I welcomed the opportunity to perform accordingly.

Full Jails

I don't think people know this so I'm reporting it so they'll have a little better understanding why sometimes judges have to suspend a sentence when the people think we should be a little more stringent, a little more severe and punish these people a little more harshly.

You see on occasion from time to time the warden at the penitentiary calls us and tells us not to send any more prisoners to the penitentiary because they don't have any room for them and that's a fact and that's what happens. I found that especially happens with reference to women. They must have very limited resources to accommodate women prisoners because frequently during the year we get a call telling us, "No more women prisoners. We don't have room for them." I think people should understand that's what happens and maybe they'll understand why when we round up a bunch of prostitutes we suspend the sentence--we cannot send them to the penitentiary because there's no more room for them.

Reluctant Playground Counselors

Another thing I didn't expect, on occasion when some of the kids got into trouble or difficulty, I thought it would be a good idea if I recommended that they be turned over to the Director of the Tigers AC. The Tigers AC organization ran athletic programs, baseball, softball, basketball and touch football. They had a nice athletic program going on all summer long to accommodate the kids and the kids all enjoyed it. Well, I thought that maybe these kids that got in trouble on occasion would find some help by joining up with the rest of the kids that were behaving themselves.

Surprisingly, the director called me on the phone and said, "Don't send me those bad boys. I don't want them in my group. I've not these nice boys, behaving themselves, doing what they're supposed to, enjoying themselves. I don't want them spoiled, tarnished or led astray by these delinquents." I said, "Mr. Jones, (name fictitious) that's why you got that program. That's why people like me support your program so you can keep kids out of trouble. What I'm sending you are boys and girls for that matter who have been in trouble but not too often--or maybe never more than once at all, I want them to go and join a group where they're having fun, enjoying themselves and staying out of trouble. That's your purpose and that's my purpose and I'm saying to you, you'd better be sure to take these kids under your wing, help straighten them out, keep an eye on them and make sure they show up and do what they're supposed to. If, by any chance, any of the boys I send to you-- or girls--turn out, unfortunately, as bad apples, let me know. I don't want your kids being spoiled or affected in any way wrongfully by the ones I send you. But I hope and pray that once these boys get under your tutelage and under your supervision they will turn out okay, behave themselves and become good, solid citizens. Take my word for it. This is probably a good solution to a problem that bothers me. I don't want these kids turning out to be criminals.

Poker Playing Wife

This is a matter that amused me no end. This fellow was a DPW, that is a displaced person who had come to America, I guess, because they had made arrangements for him to come to America but he didn't quite understand American ways.

He came to me because his wife, I believe on Friday nights--she worked by the way for the telephone company as a cleaning woman--and on Friday nights after they cleaned the ladies went to one of the women's houses and they played a little poker. I guess that was their entertainment. It wasn't much of a poker game, a nickels and dimes affair. But anyway, that was sort of entertainment and instead of getting home around 9:30 or 10:00 o'clock she'd make it home around 12:00.

Her husband came to see me because he said he kept telling her she can't do that; that she has gotta come home straight after work and she cannot go play poker.

He said "card play." I got a kick out of that. But anyway I said to him, "Does your wife use any of the money you give her to run the house in these poker games." He said, "No, she works at the telephone company and if she loses any money it's only a few dollars. It's her money. She doesn't use any of my money. If she has any money left over that I give her to run the house, we put it in the bank in our joint name." I said, "Mr. Jones, let me explain something to you. Your wife works, she earns money, and with that money she plays a little poker once a week with the ladies and she enjoys herself. This is America. You can't tell her she can't do that. She has a right to do what she does because she has the freedom to do certain things here in America that probably you were able to dictate to her that she couldn't do when you were over in the Ukraine. But at any rate, I can't tell her she can't go play poker on Friday nights and you can't stop her, be that as it may. Make the most of it. You watch your daughters until she gets home and I'm sure this will be a lot better for both of you." He looked at me and he said, "That be the law, your honor?" I said, "Yes, that's the law. Your wife has certain privileges, certain rights and you cannot ignore them." So he made the sign of the cross and said, "In the name of the Father, name of the Son, and name of the Holy Ghost, God bless America."

Horse Betting Wife

It was rather funny that I should have that case about the poker playing wife of the DPW because about a month later another DPW guy came in to see me and wanted me to stop his wife from going to Vernon Downs, a race track.

It seems that occasionally on a Saturday night his wife who also worked in the telephone company as a cleaning woman, and some other women would take the bus and go off to Vernon Downs which was only about twelve miles away and play the horses. He wanted me to stop her from going to play the horses. I said, "John, (name fictitious), your wife works in the telephone company?" He said, "Yes." "Does she use any of the money that you give her to run the house when she goes down to Vernon Downs to play the horses?" He said, "No, she just uses that little money that she loses on the horses, she uses the money that she earns from the telephone company." So I said, "Does she neglect her housework? Does she fail to provide you with a meal those nights? Does she fail to clean the house? Does she fail to do the dishes? Does she fail to make the beds? In other words, does she fail to do what she's supposed to do as a housewife?" "Oh, no", he said, "Your honor, she do good, she good wife. I don't like she go Vernon Downs. I no like she go play horses. I think she find something else to do besides she go on Saturday nights and I don't want her go on Saturday nights to play horses." Well, I told him the same thing. I said, "This is America, your wife has certain freedoms, certain privileges, certain rights. You can't tell her she can't go to Vernon Downs to play the horses." "I no can tell her that?" He said, "That's right. You cannot tell your wife she can't do that. You may tell her you don't like it, you may tell her you wish she didn't, but you can't stop her from going. If she uses only the money that she gets from the telephone company to play the horses, doesn't use any house money, and doesn't do anything that detracts from her housework and doing her job as a wife, she's free to go for a good time once a week or once a month down to Vernon Downs. As I understand it, they only run anyway during the summer. I think she's entitled to have some fun."

He looked me in the eye and said, That be the law?"
I said, "Yep, that's the law--you can't stop her. You'd
better make the most of it and behave yourself. Don't
lay a hand on her, don't try to beat her up. Don't try to
do anything of that kind", I said, "or I'll lock you up and
send you to jail." He reached back, made the sign of the
cross and said, "In the name of the Father, name of the
Son, name of the Holy Ghost, God bless America." I
said, "You bet."

"Do-Gooders" and Prostitution

I also would like to report that from time to time "do-gooders" would come to my office and demand we do something about the prostitution in the village. I said, "Ma am, there isn't much we can do. That's the oldest profession in history." I said, It'll go on, and on, and on and there's nothing we can do about it." "Well", she said "Why don't you send them to jail for a year and if they go to jail for a year they probably won't be out in the street pedaling their wares?" I said, "That wouldn't be fair. We can't just send somebody to jail for a whole year for violation of a statute which in the eyes of the law is not really that serious a crime. They are not really committing a crime. It's on the statute books, it's called a crime, they can be arrested for it. But, you know, stamping out prostitution is difficult.

I'll tell you what we'll do. I'm going to talk to the Chief of Police and we're going to send some policemen out there on these various corners where these prostitutes are plying their wares. We're going to bring them in here and charge them with prostitution. See if that may help. I don't know. It could help, but we'll see."

So a couple days later the police went down and they rounded up about three, four, or five of these prostitutes and brought them up in front of me. I got their names, got their addresses--they all lived in the same house. I asked the Village Chief of Police, "Where's the pimp? Where's the guy that hires these girls, puts them out on the street to sell their wares?" He said, "Well, we don't have any pimps here." I said, "Pretty Good. We're supposes to stop prostitution but the only people we arrested are prostitutes. The pimps go free."

Anyway, the girls were represented by an attorney and the attorney moved to have the cases adjourned, pleaded "not guilty"; so here we were--three or four more cases on the calendar which is already crowded and certainly we wouldn't be able to reach these cases for another three or four months. But, that's the law. He has a right to plead "not guilty" and he has a right to have an adjournment and we have the obligation of fixing a time for trial. So, the cases were adjourned. That was the way it was handled that morning.

The next night, I said to the police, "Go down to those corners and see what you see." "What for, your honor?" "Because I have a strong hunch, a strong feeling, that if you go down to those corners where you found these prostitutes, you'll find some more." Sure enough, they went down to those corners where those girls were plying their wares, here they were, three others, all selling their bodies. They asked me at the time, "Should we arrest them?" I said, "No, don't bother because the pimp will just put three or four more out there. If you can find the pimp, and catch him, go ahead and bring him in."

I forgot to mention that when the girls were brought in front of me, I took them into my office one by one to question them why? What are you doing out there? Why are you selling your body? and, most of all, how about telling me who your pimp is, where he lives, what's his name and so forth?" Each one of the prostitutes looked at me and chuckled. "His name is Tony. And if we can't tell you where he lives, how he could be reached, we don't know. He never tells us where he lives, never tells us where he goes, never tells us anything. He just tells us where to go to work, and we give him the money at the end of the day. And believe me, your honor, if we did know where he lived and told you, we'd probably find ourselves at the bottom of Onondoga Lake. That's the business."

I said, "Well, tell me, why are you a prostitute?" "Well", she said "I'll tell you, your honor, I came home at 2:00 o'clock in the morning one night only that one time. My father was terribly upset, called me a whore, told me to pack my suitcase, put my clothes in a suitcase and get out. Here I was out in the street, no shelter, no job, no money, no nothing. I'm walking down the street. I run into this girl, telling her about my plight and she said 'Why don't you come with me? I think we can do something for you.' Well, what they did for me was to take me into this home and I became a prostitute. I think, your honor, you'll find that almost all of us girls who ply our trade have similar situations. We don't have a job, don't have an education, don't have shelter and this is about the only thing we can do and really we don't have any help. One of my friends here doesn't even have a father. He deserted them a long time ago and she's a prostitute because that's the only way she can make any money to live, to help pay the bills. So you see, your honor, we're not enjoying this, we don't enjoy selling our bodies for money but we find ourselves pretty much in a pickle. Either do something like this, or starve to death, or sleep out in the cold weather, no shelter. That's about the way it is.'

I found out for the most part when I discussed these things with the prostitutes that were picked up, that was always the same sad story. No alternative, nothing available for them but prostitution. That's why it's so prevalent and that's why it's going to be hard to wipe out.

Bribes

Another thing that happens frequently and I think I should report is the matter of bribes. Being elected Police Court Judge meant that I was, of course, one of the few officers elected to office and for some reason or other contractors and people who wanted to do business with the village seemed to think that I had a lot of influence with the mayor and the board and I could exercise that and help them get these contracts.

They would come in to see me and say to me, "You know the mayor, you know people on the board because you ran with them in the office and certainly they belong to your party. We'd like you to see to it that we get this contract, or we get this chance to make a deal with the village." I'd look at them and say, "I don't have that much influence. I'll put in a good word for you if you want me to but that's about as far as I go." They'd say, "No, we don't want you to just do this for nothing.

We want to pay you, give you a little something for your effort." I said, "You mean you want to bribe me?" "Well, you can call it that, but it's not really a bribe. It's just that we want to give you a little something to make sure that you'll help us get these contracts. And it's not unusual," they'd say to me, "almost every place we go all over the state we always have to cough up some money or we don't get the contract. As a matter of fact, what we really want to make sure is that if we're the low bidder, we get the contract and somebody else who's the high bidder doesn't get it because he managed to 'take care' of the ones who could help." I said, "Well, I'm sorry, but I worked awfully hard to get to where I am. It cost a lot of money for my education, I became a lawyer, I got elected judge and I'm not going to have somebody come in here and offer me some money to make sure that they get a contract or not." I said, "If you got a good contract and you're going to do the job well and you come here as the low bidder, I'm sure the board here in this village, and the mayor who has some influence, will see to it that you get the contract."

He looked at me and he said, "What are you? Averse to a little something for helping us out?" I said, "I'll tell you what, you come in here with $100,000 and maybe I'll think about it because you know with $100,000 I don't have to worry about this job. In fact, I probably don't have to do much practicing law. But, no mister, if you come in as a low bidder, I promise you that you will get the contract. We're a new group, newly elected to office and we've made up our mind that we're not going to go for any of this foolishness that we think has been going on before. So, come in with your bids, submit them and be prepared to do the job properly. If you don't have the equipment, if you don't have the reputation of doing the job right, you won't get the contract. Okay thanks for coming in, sorry, I'll do what I can to help you by just telling them what I first said but I warn you, you're not going to be considered unless you can do the job properly and unless you come in with the low bid.

Speeding School Kids

The principal of the school had called me saying he wanted something done about all these kids, especially the boys, who at noon time jump in their cars, dash off wherever they went, then race back to school, speeding on Hazard Street, failing to stop for any stop sign which is at the intersection of Hazard and Concord. In other words, racing down past the school, into the parking lot and just about making it back to school in time for classes.

He said, "Not only am I upset about all this racing and car running but the people on Hazard Street are upset because the kids are exceeding the speed limit by more than 10 or 15 miles an hour and dashing down the street in a hurry to get to school." I said, "Well, I think you're right, I think we oughta do something about it. I'll tell you what to do. Tomorrow send a couple of policemen out there and when these kids come speeding down Hazard Street,--fail to stop for the sign, have them give them a ticket. And, by the way, once these policemen stop them, I want them to check the cars too. There's about 17 different items in the motor vehicle law for which a driver or owner of a vehicle can be responsible: Lack of a windshield wiper, or lack of a windshield, no emergency brake, lights that don't work, horn that doesn't blow. There are about 16 items. Tell the police to check every car that is being driven by those kids to make sure that they are not in violation of any one of those other sections of the vehicular traffic law. Lets make this a goodie."

Sure enough the next morning I had 14 boys and one girl in front of me, all who received tickets. Included among the 14 boys was my nephew. My brother walked to work, which wasn't too far, so that his son could have a car to drive to school like the rest of those boys, race around after the morning session, jump in the car, dash over wherever they were going, then race back speeding down Hazard Street to get to school on time. I had the clerk take their name and if they didn't own the car ascertain the name of the owner who for the most part turned out to be their father or mother. And so after we took all this information down, I took each one of the boys and the girl separately and said, "According to the information here you are not only charged with speeding, but you don't have a windshield wiper on your car. That means your father, the owner of this vehicle, is also guilty of a violation. So before I dispose of this case, we're going to have to have him here." Next boy, I said, "After I read the information for speeding," I said, "according to the information here you don't have an emergency brake on your car. You don't own the car but your father does, so he's going to have to appear because there's a vehicle traffic violation here."

Then I took the next case. I said to the young man, You've been charged with speeding but I notice here from the information that you didn't have a horn on your vehicle. And the police have found that you had no operable horn and that's a violation of a section of the vehicular traffic law, so your father is going to have to appear."

I took the next boy, told him he was charged with speeding and I said, "According to the information here, there doesn't seem to be any tail light that's working properly. That's a violation of one of the sections of the vehicular traffic law so you'd better have your father here on the adjourned date that I fix after we finish here."

Then I talked to the next boy, read him that he was charged with speeding and told him according to the information here from the police officer, "Your car did not have headlights. I know it was daylight; but, nevertheless, you cannot drive a car without headlights. And, I want your father here with you on the adjournment date."

I talked to the next boy. I said, "You're charged with speeding and I don't find from the information here that you have anything wrong with the car so there aren't any further charges but I want your father here anyway on this adjourned date."

I talked to the next boy, told him he was charged with speeding and I also told him that he didn't have proper brakes, brakes that would stop the car within the certain distance. According to the vehicle law, that was a violation. And I went on and I charged the other two boys and the girl with speeding and I told them I wanted them to appear on the adjourned date.

I said to all of them, "You kids have the privilege of driving your car to school. I am sure the Chief of Police and almost all the officers here--had to walk to school--and here you violate the privilege by speeding and by running off during the noon hour, God knows where, and then not getting back in time so you have to speed down Hazard Street, scare the devil out of the people, don't stop for the stop sign, and create havoc so that the principal had to call the Chief of Police and complain. Now we're going to stop this. We're not going to have this happen anymore. One thing for certain, I'm going to tell the principal of the school that you do not have parking privileges on the school grounds and you're not going to park these cars out in the street because you can't park them in the parking lot; because if you do, we're going to pick up the car and your father is gonna be pretty upset if he has to go to some garage where the car was towed and pay a towing bill. Now hear me clearly and hear me straight-forward, you're not going to be running up and down Hazard Street having a merry, good time. You are school kids, you should be in school when you're supposed to be and you shouldn't have to be speeding in the village to get to school or to get to your classes.

On the adjourned date, I fined all of those who had speeding tickets, $10 fine. The fathers who owned the cars, I said, "You'd better get these things fixed. There is no official charge against you, it's just that the police wanted you to know at my instructions that your cars were not in keeping with laws of this state as far as equipment is concerned. So I'm telling you now, be sure to get those things straightened out and fixed, windshield wipers, emergency brake, lights, etc. I'm not going to charge you officially now with any of those violations; but believe me, if your car is involved, or you are involved, or your kids are involved in another violation and these things have not been taken care of, I'm going to charge you with a violation of the vehicular traffic laws." "And you," I said to my brother, "I hate to think that you have to walk to and from work so that your kid can drive your car to school and he only lives about one-quarter of a mile, or an eighth of a mile from school. Let him walk, and you take your car to and from work. I don't want to hear about this kind of nonsense any more."

Indecent Exposure

This next case was one I am reporting only because the circumstances were such that I thought of giving a message to the parents about their children, especially their daughters.

It seems that this veteran Marine who had fought in Guadalcanal was standing in the parlor of his house with a big picture window facing the street and he beckoned these two girls to come into the house and sort of indicated he would give them each a bottle of Pepsi Cola or Coca Cola. It seems from the information that the girls went into the house and he went over to the refrigerator supposedly to pick up a couple of bottles of Pepsi and give it to the girls. But when he got halfway to the refrigerator, he turned to the girls and flagged his dick. I don't know what he intended to do. I don't know whether he knew what he intended to do, but he had been discharged from the Marine Corps because he was a Section Eight they call it. So chances are he didn't know for sure what he was doing.

The mothers of these two girls; oh, by the way, the two girls, they looked at this man, dashed out the door, ran home and told their mother about it. The mother came out to the police station and wanted a warrant sworn out against this gentleman for indecent exposure which, of course, was what had happend.

I had the man brought before me, read the charge and told him that he was entitled to have a lawyer, told him he was entitled to have his case tried before a jury, if he wished, which he did. On the adjourned date he came with his attorney and we set it down for trial.

Meanwhile, I called the two mothers in to my office and said to them, "You really don't want to pursue this case do you? I mean, you really don't want the prosecution to go on and prosecute this fellow for indecent exposure which, of course, happened in his house?" And the mother said, "What difference does it make? He exposed himself and he exposed himself to our daughters. We don't know what he intended to do, but he ought to be punished for what he did." I said, "All well and good, but remember when this case unfolds your daughters are going to have to say on the stand that they voluntarily walked into his house because he beckoned to them. Now the public is entitled to be there at a trial and chances there'll be somebody there to listen to this trial because if they hear about it, they'll know it's going to be a trial of some interest. Now do you want your daughters to get on the stand and testify that they're walking down the street and some guy in a window beckons them to come into the house and they do so? Tell me, don't you find that unusual? Don't you find that somewhat unsatisfactory? Do you wish to have people in this village learn that your two daughters walked into a strange house because they were beckoned to come into the house and didn't they know, or shouldn't they have known, that it wouldn't be right for them to walk into a house where they saw a man, whom they didn't know. Don't you teach these girls, don't you tell these girls how they should conduct themselves with reference to strangers, especially men who wish for them to come into the house and for what reason? Okay, if you want to pursue this case, go ahead; but I'm telling you now, it isn't going to look good and I'm also telling you that this lawyer who represents this fellow might very well use this to point out that his client, the defendant, who was discharged from the Marine Corps after fighting in Guadalcanal was a Section Eight, that he isn't 100 per cent all there and secondly he's going to probably point out to the jury that what did these two girls expect going into a house where they were beckoned by a stranger to come in for some goodies or something and not know what risks they were taking by doing so." One mother looked at the other and said, "Well, what do you think? It doesn't look too well does it? If we push for a prosecution we have no way of knowing who might be in the court room listening to the trial and certainly it wouldn't be nice to have people in the village find out that we have a couple of daughters who don't know enough to mind their own business when they're out in the public and actually walk into this house just because some strange man beckons them to come in and was going to offer them something like a bottle of Coke or Pepsi Cola, I don't think it's gonna look too well," she said. The other mother said, "I kinda agree with you, so I think we had better ask that this case be dismissed and, well, maybe the judge will do something about this man anyway because he shouldn't be allowed to do what he did either" The other mother said to the judge, who was myself, "I think we'll talk to the District Attorney and tell him not to pursue this case but we want you to do something about this man. We don't think he should have beckoned the girls to come into the house and we don't think he should have been doing what he did. He's really guilty of indecent exposure. I suppose that if he did it in his own house, it's not as bad as if he did it out in the street somewhere; but, at any rate, you'll have to do something. You'll have to talk to him about this and tell him he shouldn't do it again and tell him why we're dismissing the case. We're not going to prosecute the case." I said, "You have my word that I'll do my level best to make sure that he doesn't get away with anything like this again."

They told the District Attorney that they didn't want the case prosecuted, and I had the young man come in to my office and I lectured really strongly about his conduct and I said to him, "I want you to make an appointment with a psychiatrist and I want that psychiatrist to know that I ordered you to go to him and I'm going to have you tell that psychiatrist what you did and I'm going to have to see why, find out from the psychiatrist what caused you to perform that indecent act. Believe me, when you're through with the psychiatrist, when you're through with whatever it is that you have to do, that he recommends in the way of your future behavior, don't you ever come before me again with a matter of this kind because you are going to 'sail', understand?" He said, "Yes, your honor, I don't know what got into me. I don't know why I did what I did, but you can rest assured I'll see a psychiatrist and maybe he can tell me what's wrong with me and tell me why I did what I did. You can be assured that I'll never do anything like that again."

Misplaced Urine Sample

This next case involved a drunken driving case and it appears that on the day of trial, the urine sample that was taken from the defendant was sent to Camillus. It wasn't sent to my office where the Assistant District Attorney would be able to use the urine sample in evidence to prosecute his case. The District Attorney told me that the sample that he needed in reference to the case involved was needed to prosecute the case had not been sent to my office but had been sent to Camillus.

Of course, I know and he knew what a Defense Attorney would do with evidence of that kind. You see the whole case depends upon what the lab tests show with reference to the alcohol in the urine then that's translated to determine how much alcohol was in the blood stream and then, of course, that determines the culpability. Well, you have to be sure that these samples are not tampered with. You have to be sure that they are under control at all times by the authorities. Certainly if a sample and the evidence, that is the lab tests from the sample, are sent to another jurisdiction, the defense lawyer is going to raise havoc with that evidence and we're not going to be able to get a verdict. So, I agreed with the District Attorney that, under the circumstances, it would be wise to dismiss the case before we're all embarrassed by the fact that the sample was sent to another jurisdiction.

Tainted Evidence

Along that line I had another case involving drunken driving in which it was proven during the trial that the sample which was taken, that is the urine sample, to determine the degree of the amount of alcohol in the blood stream of the defendant, it was not put away under lock and key and kept under surveillance so that it would be untarnished evidence of the defendant's guilt.

This sample was left, according to the testimony, on a counter in the police station in the sheriffs office all night long and, of course, the Defense Attorney made a lot of noise about that because with a sample out on the counter all night before it is tested, it is really subject to any kind of tampering. Just a little bit of alcohol that could have been dropped into the sample would prove disastrous to the defendant. At any rate it turned out that the District Attorney, when he heard that evidence, moved to have the case dismissed because he said the evidence was tarnished and he didn't think the jury would come out with a verdict of guilt under the circumstances.

I mention that in this book, these two cases, because I want to be sure that people know that any evidence that is taken to determine whether or not a person is actually guilty of drunken driving must be carefully guarded and watched over so that it cannot be tampered with because it is so easy to tarnish a sample sitting on a bench in a police station or in a sheriffs department. All someone has to do is drop a very small, minuscule amount of alcohol in that sample to ensure that the defendant will be proven guilty. We don't tolerate that in our courts. We want to be sure that there is no reasonable doubt because actually a charge of driving while intoxicated is very serious.

So I mention that as a couple of cases in which the prosecution, the police, all those involved have to be very careful what they do with the evidence and how they safeguard it so it won't be subject to some kind of doubt that will be raised, certainly, by the Defense Lawyer.

Wife Beating

The next case involves a case in which the husband was brought up before me because he had beaten his wife and he was charged, of course, with "Assault Third Degree."

I had told the police when I took office that before I became judge there was a case in which the police had been called to the house and there was a fight going on, or had gone on, and the husband had beaten the wife and the police thought they had solved the problem, settled the argument and left. They left the man there in the house with the wife whom he had just beaten. It turned out that after the police had left and left him there with his wife, I guess the argument started over again; he ended up shooting and killing his wife. I told the police when I took office, I don't want anything like that happening on my beat. If you're called, I said, at any time because there's a fight going on and it turns out the

87

man, the husband, has laid his hands on the woman or beaten her, you're not to leave that house without him. Take him with you and lock him up. The police said, "What are we going to charge him with?" I said, "Take him with you and lock him up. I'm not going to have him sitting there waiting for you to leave, start the fight all over again, and then have something like that happen on my beat. So just take him to the police station and lock him up. I'll figure out something in the morning. I don't have any problem. He's half drunk, he'll be half drunk when he gets there and he'll be almost drunk when he comes up before me in the morning.

"When I tell him what had happened he's going to be shocked because he's going to be told he could very well, this time, be sent to the penitentiary for a good long period." You see, before I became judge several of these men who had beaten their wives had records of same. I made it my business to make sure that if any of these fellows who had beaten their wives should come before me, they're not going to do it again.

So in this case when the man came up before me after they brought him upstairs from the cell, I told him what had happened and I asked him how did he plead? He said, "Plead to what?" I said, "Wife beating, assault third degree. You're entitled to a lawyer, of course, you're entitled to a trial; but at this time his wife who was in the court room came up and said, "May I say something, your honor? I said, "Sure, go ahead, you're the complainant, go ahead." She said, "I'd like to withdraw the complaint. I don't want my husband prosecuted." I said, "Young lady, you don't have a right to withdraw the complaint. This case is not a case of you versus your husband. This is a case as are all cases of criminal nature--it's always a case of The People of The State of New York against the defendant-and that's so in this case. You're not the people of The State of New York; the people of The State of New York are the ones who will be prosecuting this case, so you can't withdraw this complaint." "Well", she said "if I don't withdraw the complaint, he'll have to stand trial won't he?" I said, "Yep, that's about the size of it," and I said, "Lady, he beat you up once before but I want to apprise you right now, he'll never do it again because when I get through with him, believe me, he'll think twice before he gets himself in this kind of a mess again." She said, "I know, but don't I have to come here and testify against him?" I said, "Yes." She said, "Well then he's really gonna be mad at me and then there'll be hell to pay." I said, "No there won't, no there won't. I'm the judge in this case and I'm giving him an opportunity to think about it. If he wants to hire a lawyer, he can hire a lawyer, if he doesn't want a lawyer, he could come here without a lawyer, but when I get through with this matter, you can rest assured this no good, wife beater husband of yours isn't going to get away with it again. So this case is adjourned for one week and I turned to the man and said, "Don't you for one moment think that you're going to get away with anything because the other time that it happened your wife came up here and withdrew the charge. She is not entitled to withdraw the charge. The State of New York has to make that decision and the State of New York is me and the District Attorney. So don't you go back home and start this argument all over again and don't you go back home and lay a hand on your wife because if you do my friend, young man, you're going to 'sail' and I mean 'sail' for a long time and when you get out of that penitentiary I don't think you'll want to go fooling around with monkey business such as this like beating your wife. So I'm telling your wife right now that if you go home if you start any argument with her because she called the police and you got locked up, she's to call the police. I'm telling the police that when they go there, they are to grab you, put you in the patrol car, take you over here and lock you up and tomorrow morning, whatever the time, you're not going to get the opportunity to do it again. This is going to stop in this village as long as I am the judge. So hear me out, come in here and you'd better make sure you behave yourself." I didn't have to send this wife beater to jail--I just locked him up weekends-and, believe me, he learned his lesson.

False Report

This case I'm reporting because I think it should be of some interest to parents to understand what can happen under certain circumstances and they shouldn't get all excited about something that they're told by their kids.

You see, these two girls who were supposed to be home by 4:00 o'clock on this given day didn't get home 'til 6:00 o'clock. So I think, I'm not sure, but I think they cooked up this story to get their parents excited and so that the parents certainly would forget that they didn't get home when they were supposed to.

The facts of the case are as follows: The girls told their fathers that they were coming home the short-cut way through the park. Part of the park has a wooded area and they said that when they were coming through the park in the wooded area, this man who had exposed himself, was chasing them trying to catch them. They said that they ran as fast as they could, got out of the woods, got down to the street, got home and escaped being caught by the man who was in the woods. Of course, the fathers got all excited about that, called the police and wanted this person, whomever he was, apprehended and charged with some kind of crime for chasing the girls and exposing himself. So the police went up there into the woods and searched all over and the only thing they found was this old man about 85 or 86 years old sitting on the bench smoking his pipe.

They went over to him and asked him if he had seen anything in the nature of some fellow chasing girls or something of that kind. He said, "No, but he did remember seeing two girls coming up in back." They said, "What did you notice about these girls?" He said, "Well, I noticed they were walking down the path, I was over by the tree over there and I was peeing and I guess that kinda got them excited and nervous because when I turned around to see who it was, I didn't cover myself up. I don't know what they were thinking but they took off like a bullet and that's about as much as I know of it and I haven't seen anybody around here. I think I'm about the only one that's been here in the woods all this while. If those girls claim they saw somebody chasing them, it certainly couldn't be me because I can hardly walk, least of all try to catch somebody."

When I got there the police told me the story and he said, "Go and talk to the old gent." I did and he told me the same thing and I listened to him and I sort of suspected that there was something fishy here. I asked for the girls to come into my office, they were out in the court room. I talked to them and I explained to them that this old man was in the woods, he admitted that he saw them and he admitted that he was, at the time you girls cam upon him, it sort of frightened him too because he was peeing up against the tree and when he turned obviously he exposed himself and you girls were obviously upset. I said, "Now you know this old man certainly, if he's the one you saw in the woods, certainly wasn't able to chase you down the path out of the woods." One girl said, "Was this man wearing a blue shirt and brown khaki pants?" I said, "Yes, that's the garb." "Well, I guess that was the fellow alright but we didn't know, we were scared and we weren't sure he couldn't run and that's why we did what we did." "Yes, I said but you also told your parents that this man chased you out of the woods. Now he didn't chase you anywhere and you told your fathers because you were getting home late and you thought you'd get them so excited about what had happened that they'd forget all about the fact that your should have been home at 4:00 o'clock." Well, the girls kind of looked down at the floor a little sheepishly, didn't answer but I gathered that what I'd said had been pretty much the case.

Boys and girls and fathers I hope you learn something from this and you fathers not to get so excited every time the girls tell you something, you right away want to call the police and check out somebody to see if somebody can be apprehended and charged with a crime when no such thing had happened. So be careful in the future. Make sure you get your stories straight and make sure that your daughters aren't covering their tracks in some way.

Then I turned to the girls and I said, "Did you learn something from this?" One girl said, "Yes, we have. Number one, we had better be truthful because it'll be found out that we weren't telling the truth and Number two, whenever we come home from any place wherever we may be, we'd better not go home through the woods because it didn't happen now but something serious could happen." I turned to the other girl and I said, "What about you?" She said, "I agree, we should have stayed on the streets, the long way home where people are located and there is little chance of being apprehended or caught or for that matter, raped.

So I guess we learned to stay away from the woods and stay away from places where things seriously can happen." I said, "Good and remember also, try to go wherever you go in groups. At least two of you. Number one. Number two, don't get into any car with any stranger, ever, because that could lead to trouble. Number three, if someone beckons you from the window of his house to come into the house, don't go in there. Don't go into any house, any time, anywhere because someone beckons you. And that applies to whether or not its somebody you know or don't know. Just don't find yourselves in a position where you go into somebody's house at any time because bad things can happen. Now do you hear me?" The girls said, "Yes, your honor, we understand." I said, "You girls are vulnerable. There are sex maniacs out there and you're always going to be in danger, so watch out, be careful, don't get yourself in a position where you might be attacked. Please, we don't want anything to happen to you, so don't let yourself get exposed."

PART TWO

I am now going to turn to the second part of my book. I have selected a number of cases which I selected and I really believe they will be of interest and/or humorous to the reader. As Police Court Judge, I presided over thousands of cases and I have selected those which I thought would be of greater interest and which would be the most humorous to the reader. I will start off by indicating the cases by number. (Case one Tape) I have decided that this would be part two of my book, so I discuss these various cases which I selected which I thought would be of great interest and in many instances humorous.

Case One
Speeding Ticket

In open court session this morning, a Marine Lieutenant appeared before me in full regalia; full uniform, ribbons and all. He was charged with speeding 35 miles an hour in the village which has a speed limit of 25 miles per hour. I asked him if he had that same uniform on when the policeman gave him the ticket. He said, "No." They are allowed to wear civilian clothes, he said, when on leave, and he was on leave for two weeks. I said, "So I see. You were in civilian clothes when the policeman gave you that ticket." "That's right," he said." Well, do you have an explanation for the speed that you were traveling 35 miles in a 25 miles per hour speed zone?" "Well, to tell the truth Judge" he said, "I fly fighter planes at the speed of to 450 miles per hour. When I got home and got into my car and had myself limited to 35 miles per hour I really thought I was standing still because of the difference in the speeds. But I was speeding, and I want to plead guilty." I said, "Lieutenant, your explanation as to why you were going as fast as you were at the time is satisfactory to me. Case dismissed."

Case Two
Sleeping With the Dogs

This drunk had been picked up during the night, locked up because he was causing such a disturbance in the neighborhood, so when he appeared in front of me, I, which I generally do, asked him how he pleaded. He said, "I think I have to plead guilty because I was making a lot of noise and I was disturbing the peace, I guess, but I have an excuse for doing so." So, I said, "Go ahead, what's your excuse?" He said, "How would you like it if your wife told you to go sleep with the dog." I hesitated for a moment, gave thought to what he said and I replied. "What kind of a dog was it?" This brought a lot of chuckles from the people in the court room. I was told the dog was a boxer and I said to the drunk, "I'm sorry, but that's not the kind of dog I would like to sleep with. The fine is $10 and you behave yourself and don't dome back here again."

Case Three
Homewrecker

It seems that this is a case that probably never should have been tried; but, at any rate, the complainant insisted that the prosecution go on against the wife of her boyfriend. The testimony at the trial wasn't very long. It seemed that for the most part what had happened was that the defendant had yanked the complainant out of her husband's car, dragged her to the ground and was in the process of beating her, when her husband came out of the house and separated the two women. The husband, who was now separated from his wife, had come to the house that day with some Christmas presents that he wanted to give to the kids; and, while he was in the house his girlfriend was sitting in the car out there in the driveway.

The defendant testified that she had told this woman, the complainant, never to come on her property again. She said, "You stole my husband away from me and my kids and I never want to see you again least of all I don't want to see you on my property." Apparently, the complainant said nothing. That made the defendant even more angry. That's when she reached in, grabbed the complainant by the head of the hair and pulled her out onto the pavement in the driveway. That was pretty much the testimony throughout the trial; the jury seemed to be quite attentive and they were listening to the testimony pretty carefully.

One thing that happened, however, was that the defense attorney, when he finished summing up the trial turned to the jury and he said, "Ladies and Gentlemen of the Jury you've heard testimony in this trial. You learned how the complainant stole the defendant's husband away from her and the children. You can understand why she was so angry at the time. All I have to say is, she made one simple mistake. She should have gone out there with a baseball bat and hammered away at that girl, the complainant here who stole her husband."

The jury took the case and was only gone about 15 minutes and came out and said, "We find the defendant 'not guilty' and we believe that what the defense lawyer said ought to be in vogue; she should have used a baseball bat." In fact, the facts were pretty limited.

Case Four
The Reluctant Juror

All I remember about the case was that the jury got the case about 10:00 o'clock that evening and they were gone for some time. Surprisingly enough it was at least two hours before they knocked on the door to let us know that they were ready to render a decision. When they came into the courtroom and sat down I asked them if they had rendered a decision? and they said that "No, they hadn't." The foreman looked over at this one woman indicating, of course, that the reason they couldn't come to a decision was because she was the one holding things up. So, I said, "The hour is late, I gather that you have reached pretty close to a decision, probably five to one." He nodded his head. I said, "Why don't you go back, spend a little more time, review the evidence and see if you can't come up with an agreement so we won't have to try this case all over again." He acceded to my wish, they went back to the deliberation room and five minutes later came back, and I thought I guess they have reached a decision-- convinced that lady to go along with the rest of the five. I asked the foreman, "Have you reached a verdict?" He said, "No we haven't, your honor." I said, "What?" He said, "No, your honor, we convinced the lady over here who stood for a not guilty verdict and when we voted again, she, we thought, had been convinced, but the vote was still five to one." So, I turned to the lady whom I thought we had convinced and she said, "Wait a minute, I voted for a conviction, I'm not the one holding up this trial;" and, another lady raised her hand and said, "Your Honor, I didn't like the idea that they practically forced this lady to change her mind so I voted for acquittal." Well, I could see that we were not going to have any agreement on this trial, so I dismissed the jury and called it a hung jury. It never got tried again, which is usually the case.

Case Five
Nonexistent Stop Sign

This case was interesting only because it involved only me and the policeman who had given the ticket out to the defendant. I thought it was odd because the summons for the defendant to appear in court was only because he was charged with failure to stop for a stop sign. I thought it was odd, as I said, because he had pleaded not guilty and he was there with his attorney ready to try the case.

It turned out, when I listened to the evidence that the policeman admitted that at one time before he issued the ticket at least, he was watching this intersection and he noticed the defendant approaching the stop sign. He did testify, however, that at one time he took his eye off the defendant because another car was coming in the opposite direction and he wanted to make sure that he wouldn't be hit by this car. But, at any rate, he admitted on the stand that he had taken his eye off the defendant for a matter of a few seconds. I found the defendant "Not guilty" and the reason why I found him "Not Guilty", was because the policeman had not kept his eye on the defendant all the while that the thing was happening.

"It is conceivably possible", I said, that there is 'reasonable doubt' that the defendant probably did stop for the stop sign and the policeman didn't see it because he looked elsewhere." Under the circumstances, I felt the defendant should not be found guilty of the charge, so I dismissed it.

The follow-up was that the policeman waited out in the hall and asked me if the defendant was a friend, and that was why I dismissed the case. I told the policeman that, "I am bound by the same rules that we charge the jury. I have to find, if I am the sole judge and jury, that we find the defendant guilty beyond reasonable doubt. You created a reasonable doubt."

For a stop sign violation! Hired a lawyer to defend him when he pleaded not guilty. I know what lawyers charge in the way of fees when they represent people and I doubt if he hired this lawyer for less than $50. You know, you have to think if the defendant was willing to pay $50 or thereabout to defend himself, he had good sound reason to believe that he was innocent. I think that coupled with the fact that the policeman admitted, on the stand, that he took his eye off the defendant for a few seconds, constituted enough for me that there was reasonable doubt and I, therefore, dismissed the case. This policeman also said he thought that I had stretched the legal aspects of the case quite a bit in order to find the defendant not guilty.

Case Six
Wrongful Registration

He didn't like me very much after that case and I didn't think he was very competent either; because, not too long after that, he gave a defendant a ticket because he had put the little tag you get instead of a license plate--he had put that little tag on the front plate instead of the rear plate. He charged him with "wrongful registration" which is fairly harsh violation. When the defendant appeared in front of me and explained about how he had the tag on the front plate instead of the rear plate, I thought it most unusual that he should be brought before me under the circumstances. I turned to the policeman and said, "I'm going to dismiss this case because you as a policeman should also be interested in doing things that help people. Why didn't you tell this person to take the tag off the front plate and put it on the rear plate and be on his way. I'm not going to hold this man guilty for something that could have so easily remedied itself." You see, I thought that was stretching it too far.

Case Seven
Nonexistent Stop Light

There were other policemen too who didn't particularly like me because if I dismiss any case that they gave someone a summons to, they thought I was showing favoritism. In one particular case, the ticket issued to the defendant charging him with going through a street light at an intersection of First Street and Cogswell Avenue. Actually, there was no street light at that intersection. Apparently he intended to give the defendant a ticket for going through an intersection where there was a street light. I didn't think I could hold this defendant guilty for going through an intersection, charged with failure to stop for the red light when after all there wasn't one at the intersection.

The policeman who issued the ticket told me afterward that he thought I stretched things pretty far by dismissing the case. I told him that I couldn't do anything differently because he could not be charged with going through a street light where there wasn't any.

Case Eight
Wrong Date on Charge

On another occasion, a policeman gave the defendant a ticket but he put the wrong date in the summons. The defendant appeared before me and said, "Your Honor, I can prove that on the 5th of June I was working along with some other men at the Solvay Process Company. Therefore, I could not have been speeding down Milton Avenue on the 5th of June." I said, "Are you sure you can present me with witnesses here who will testify that you were working in the plant on the 5th of June.?" "Yes, Your Honor, I can do that." I believed him. I didn't think he was making up the story because if I didn't believe him and told him to present the witnesses, he knew, of course, he would bet in real trouble--not only for speeding but also for lying to the Judge. I, again, had to dismiss the case because I was satisfied that he could not have been speeding in the Village of Solvay if at the time the summons said he was, he was working in the factory.

Again, the police officer wanted to know from me why I had stretched the things a little so far as to allow this man to go free. I told the policeman I could not hold the man guilty of speeding in the Village of Solvay if he were able to prove that at the time you issued the summons and charged him with the violation, he was working in the plant. The police officer said, "Well, why didn't you adjourn the case and give me an opportunity to change the date on the summons, and correct the date and charge him with speeding at the time it took place and the day it took place." I said, "Officer, I'm only a judge, I'm not a police officer. If a person comes before me and can prove that he was not at a given spot or a given area at the time he was issued a ticket, he's not guilty of that charge. Yes, I suppose I could have said, 'This case is adjourned, and I want to give the police officer an opportunity to correct the information which is listed here on the summons'; but, I think what I want to do is teach you a lesson. You had better be accurate and you had better be clear when you make any charge against anybody it better be solidly clear that he violated the Statute or the Ordinance at the time and place you said he did. Case closed."

Case Nine
Evidence Eaten by Policemen

Another incident that I had involving the police, was very amusing, I thought, the District Attorney was getting ready to try the case against the defendant. I don't recall now what the charge was, but it was a misdemeanor; and, I think what had happened, he had stolen a ham from one of the meat markets in the village. The District Attorney came to me just before the trial and said, "Your honor, I'm going to be at a disadvantage here." He said, "Something serious has happened to this case." I said, "What happened." He said, "I talked to the police officer who made the arrest and he said he can't come here to this court and present the evidence because they ate the ham at the last PBA Meeting." I thought for a moment; well, it looks like the police ate the evidence. "If you don't have any evidence to present

117

to the jury" I said to the DA, "as to what he stole, you don't have any way to prove that he stole the ham, I guess I have nothing I can do but to dismiss the case."

So, the District Attorney appeared before me, the attorney for the defendant appeared before me. The District Attorney said, "Your honor, I move to dismiss this case because I lack the evidence to prove that he stole the item for which he's charged." He didn't mention the fact that the police had eaten the ham, he just said he lacked the evidence that he needed to prove his case. I dismissed the case and that was it.

So, you can see that sometimes, at least, the judge has to take the bull by the horns and make decisions that are not very favorable to the police. Well, the police don't like that very much. They think that every time they issue a summons or a ticket of any kind the judge should stand behind them and find the individual guilty. I try to tell them that if that were so, there would be no need for a judge. All we'd have to do is have police give out tickets or summonses and then have somebody just sit there and say, "OK, you've been charged with speeding,"--fine, $25; OK you've been charged with a misdemeanor of stealing, fine, go to the penitentiary." There would be no need for a judge to preside over the cases and make a determination as to whether a person was truly guilty or not.

I told the policeman, my role as judge was to determine beyond a reasonable doubt whether a certain person or defendant was guilty. Your job is to make the arrest and that's it. From that point on, you job is done. Leave it up to the judge to make these determinations. You don't know when sometimes I suspend sentences what the circumstances are. You police don't know when you issue a ticket that maybe this fellow has four or five kids, he's trying his best to support his family and maybe a $25 fine would be a terrible burden upon him and his family. You don't know that, but I do. I find that out and I learn what the circumstances are; and, when I suspend the sentence I am trying to make sure that his family and his kids won't suffer from the large fine that I would be imposing.

The role of a judge is that fine. He has not only to determine the guilt, he has to make sure that it is beyond a reasonable doubt. He has to make sure that it is beyond a reasonable doubt and he has to take into consideration the circumstances revolving around every single case that comes before him. Please, don't second guess me; please, don't feel as though I have done some harm to you; please, don't feel that every time you issue a ticket or summons for some violation, that I have to go ahead and punish this person with the maximum fine or send them to prison. That's not my role. That's not why people in America have judges. We do not have a dictatorship, we do not permit police to just pick somebody up, lock them up and then on his say so, fine the defendant, send him off to jail or pay a heavy fine. Your role is to arrest people that you think have violated the law, and my role is to find them guilt or innocent depending on the case and depending on the circumstances. I hope we understand each other.

Case Ten
Property Line Dispute

This case involved two neighbors it seemed who were constantly fighting over their borderline. One would plant some vegetable plants over on the other six feet and when the other fellow came home, he'd tear them up. This was going on for some time and was causing considerable trouble in the neighborhood, so the police told the two of them to come before me and see if I could resolve the situation.

I thought the solution was very simple. I said, "Why don't we get a surveyor to go over to your houses, line up the survey, you both pay half the cost, and have him straighten out the line. Apparently your line is not straight. Half of your line shows for one lot line line six feet off and the last half of the line is six feet off. The line needs to be straightened.

They wouldn't accept my solution and took their case to the Supreme Court in Onondaga County. When they finished their trial, the Supreme Court Justice decided the case the same as I had suggested two years earlier. He said, "Have a surveyor straighten out the line and quit disturing the Peace." This after spending over $1,000 in the Supreme Court--and the same soluition I offered which cost them nothing.

Case Eleven
Shoplifting

The defendant in this case was an elderly Italian woman who had been charged with shoplifting in the five and ten. When she appeared in court with her husband, I could see that she was very nervous, very upset, very frightened. As they approached the bench, when her case was called, her husband turned to her and said in Italian. "Please don't upset this judge, he is very mean and he could get very upset and, if so, he might send you to jail. So, be very careful what you say and also be careful how you act." Now, mind you, at the time he talked to his wife and told her these things in Italian there was a nameplate on my bench that said, "Donald N. Salvetti, Presiding Judge." I thought he ought to know certainly from my name that I was probably also Italian. But, he didn't.

After he told her that in Italian and I responded also in Italian and asked him where he had learned the fact that I was a mean judge. How did he come upon this kind of information. He looked me straight in the eye, turned left and right, looked back at the rest of the people in the courtroom and he said, "Hey, we got an Italian judge here. What do you know about that--hooray for our side." I found this very amusing particularly since the nameplate seemed to indicate quite plainly that I was Italian. At any rate, he didn't notice it.

The poor woman had stolen a pair of stockings worth .99 cents. I found that she had never been in trouble before, never appeared in court before, never had any problems before. So, I felt real sorry for this poor woman. I thought the manager of the store, whomever he was, should have probably figured out some way to charge her for the stockings and forget it. But he apparently wanted to make an example of this woman. I found that out certainly after the trial, after the arraignment, in fact; there hadn't been any trial. I said to the woman, "How come you stole these stocking? You know you were stealing, you know you took something you shouldn't have." She said, "Well, Judge, I have a wonderful daughter-in-law and I wanted to buy her something for Christmas, but I didn't have any money. I know I shouldn't have stolen those stockings and I know I should have told her I wanted to buy her something but couldn't afford it, but I thought maybe I could get away with it. I find now that I didn't. I'm sorry and believe me, I'm never going to get in trouble again." I said, "Well, I'm glad to hear that. You figure out some way to pay the five and dime people that .99 cents for those stockings so you could go ahead and give them as a gift to your daughter-in-law. In the meantime I'm going to adjourn this case for six months under a certain section of the law I'm permitted to do this. It's called 'Adjournment in Contemplation of Dismissal' which means in essence if you behave, don't get into any further trouble, don't do anything wrong within the next six months, you can appear here before me and I will dismiss the case. Now, don't forget. You pay the people there at the five and dime the .99 cents for the stocking. Alright!" Next case.

The manager of the five and dime came over to me and said he wanted to talk to me about the case. I said, "Fine, when I finish here well go into my office and you can discuss the matter with me." We went into the office and we no sooner sat down than he began to berate me because of the way I handled the case, especially because I dismissed it. Among other things, he went on to tell me about the great cost that these business are suffering form shoplifters, the great sums of money that are lost yearly nationwide because of shoplifters and he also told me that the only way to stop this was to make sure that those who are apprehended are promptly punished which you didn't do. I listened to him tentatively and I said, "Mr., If I fined that little old lady 25, 30, or $50, do you think that would stop the shoplifting in your store? I doubt it very much And I also doubt very much whether she'll ever be involved again in any shoplifting activity. She was terribly upset, shaking to the point where she almost collapsed in my court room and I think I did what was right.

Besides I'd like you to know that I made a study of this business of shoplifting and your loss is primarily a result of thievery that goes on by your own employees. They are the ones who do all or most of the stealing that causes you these losses--not little old ladies who steal a dollars worth of stockings. At any rate, I want you to know that the criminal code of this state provides us judges with this adjournment. I thought that this matter was one that merited the treatment that's provided by our criminal code. In other words, adjournment in contemplation of dismissal. This statute was enacted for the very purpose of permitting us judges to at times when we thought it necessary to extend some leniency in a particular case. Can you think of any other better time that I could have invoked this statute with reference to this case. If I were to ever use the statute permitting me to adjourn a case in contemplation of dismissal. This is one that I thought was most appropriate and merited that kind of attention. So, you bring before me one of your employees that you catch stealing items from your store and you'll see how differently I will probably treat that case, depending upon the circumstances of course. But at least if he's fined and punished for the act, the rest of the employees will get the message and I'm sure that message will be 'stay off, don't do the same thing your compatriot did when he stole the item.' That is not the case with this little old lady. The only people who will know that she did wrong will be her immediate family and her close friends. That's not enough to cause a great big change in shoplifting activity. So, I did what I thought was best under the circumstances. That's my job. You go back and manage your store and check on those employees who are robbing you blind. That is all, I have nothing further to say and I don't care to hear any more from you about the incident.

Case Twelve
Traveling Salesman

The next case I'm going to report resulted in a trial. The defendant it seems was a traveling salesman and he was on his way home at this time and drove by a veteran's hall where a big dance was going on--a celebration of some kind. He heard the music outside and thought he'd stop, go in and see what was going on--maybe enjoy himself somewhat.

He went into their club house, walked over to the bar and ordered himself a drink and looked around to see all the people enjoying themselves and listening to the music. Then, suddenly a young, very attractive girl came over to the bar stood next to him and said, "you're a stranger here aren't you?" He said, "Yes, I am. I just stopped in to see what was going on and maybe have a dance or two. Everything seems to be nice here, the music is fine." He said to the lady, "Can I buy you a drink?" She said, "Yes, go right ahead." So, he ordered her a drink and they were in the process of talking when the complainant came over and he said to the young lady, "Hey you, come with me, we've got to go out there and dance." She said, "I don't feel like dancing, so please, leave me alone." He grabbed her by the arm and started to drag her out onto the floor. She was protesting and insisting that she did not want to go out and dance. The defendant reached out, tried to stop him from pulling this girl out onto the dance floor. The complainant shoved the defendant back and said, "Mind your own business, this is no affair of yours. I'm going to dance with this girl and you aren't going to stop me, or anybody else." It was at this moment, while he was dragging this girl out onto the floor and she was protesting, that the defendant reached out, threw a nice, good solid sock with his fist, caught the complainant on the chin and knocked him to the floor. The girl turned to him and said, "You better get out of here because you're in deep trouble." He said, "I didn't do anything wrong. He was dragging you out onto the floor and it was about the only way I knew to stop him." She said, "I know, but he's got lot of friends here,"

At any rate, two or three of those people who were at the hall grabbed the defendant, partially really almost dragged him into the office in the back and sent for the police. The police brought him over and the next morning I arraigned him. He pleaded not guilty and we set the case down for trial.

It was an interesting trial. The facts were pretty much as I've related them. They both testified pretty much to the same thing. However, the complainant didn't admit that he was dragging the girl onto the floor, he just said he was trying to get her to go dancing with him when he got struck by the defendant. The defendant, however, told the story pretty much, I think, as it happened.

At any rate, the defense attorney reviewed the evidence for the jury. Then, he turned to the jury at the very end of his summation, and he said to the jury, "Ladies and Gentlemen of the Jury, you've heard the defendant admit that he struck the complainant and you've heard all the testimony as to how he was just in there to get a drink and you've heard the testimony about how the girl was protesting and didn't want to go out there on the floor and dance with this fellow; so, all I have to say to you is you shouldn't find him guilty because he acted like a real true blue-bloodied American boy would have acted under the circumstances. He didn't want this girl being dragged out on the floor against her will."

The jury took the case, I charged the jury, reviewed most of the evidence and I don't believe they were out more than five or ten minutes at the most. I asked them if a foreman had been elected and they said, "Yes." I said, "Alright, will the foreman please rise?" The foreman stood up and I asked him if he had a verdict? "Yes, we have a verdict." I said, "OK, what is it?" He said, "We find the defendant not guilty and we believe he did the right thing as any true-bloodied American boy would have done under the circumstances." I thanked the jury, dismissed them and told the defendant he was free to go.

Case Thirteen
Second Degree Rape

This case was very interesting, indeed. It seems that the defendant was charged with second degree rape and I was a little shocked to see this happen because he appeared like a nice guy. He didn't look like someone who would force himself on a woman.

At any rate, she told me the story. I had them both in my chambers and I was trying to talk them out of this because I had some inkling of what had happened and I didn't think the jury would probably find him guilty anyway. But, anyway I had them in my chambers and I asked the young lady--she was kind of young, maybe in her thirties--what had happened. She said, "Well, I was at this bar and I was drinking and he was buying me drinks and he started telling me about how he was going fishing in the morning and he said, "How would you like to go with me?" "Well, I figured," she said, "maybe it would be fun." "Well, the only thing is we gotta go out there on the lawn and pick up some night crawlers and use them for bait. Will you come along with me and help me find them." She said, "I don't see anything wrong with that. Sure, I'll go out." So, the two of them left the bar, went out onto the lawn and they started gathering these night worms. She said that at one point--first she said that, of course, to pick up these night crawlers you had to keep bending over. She said, "I was bending over picking up night crawlers when suddenly he came up from behind me exposed and put his dingus into me from behind. Well, I didn't like that at all. I thought that was pretty bad, and I didn't like it. I came over here to the police station, reported it to the police. They took the information, and that's how it is that he's being charged with rape second degree. I guess second degree because he didn't knock me down nor force himself on me but at any rate I think he raped me."

I turned to the fellow and I said, "Is that pretty much what happened?" He said, "Yes, your honor, we were bending over picking up these night crawlers and she kept bending over and I noticed she didn't have any pants on. I don't know what got into me but all of a sudden I did what she said I did. I really couldn't help myself. I got aroused and I did what was wrong." So, I turned to the lady and I said, "Are you going to continue to prosecute this man under those circumstances?" She said, "Why not? He had no business doing what he did to me just because he was going to take me out fishing and bought me some drinks." I said, "Yes, I know lady but under the circumstances—you were bending over and he could see pretty much that you didn't have any underpants on. Well, he got aroused and after all, he is a man and sometimes I suppose things like this can happen." "I know Judge, however, the law says 'If he penetrates me without my consent' it's rape." I stopped and thought for a minute and I said, "Lady, you are absolutely right. You didn't give consent so, in fact, he could be prosecuted if found guilty of rape. But I don't think you'll want that to happen, do you? I mean you seem friendly-the two of you don't seem like you want something like that to happen." I said, "I'll tell you what"--I turned to the defendant~I said to him, "Look, you started off okay with this young lady." She liked the fact that I kept calling her a young lady. But, I said, "You started off the night with this young lady, had a few drinks, enjoyed the conversation, I assume, then decided you were going to take her fishing. Now look at the mess you're in. So, I suggest you tell her right now that you're going to dress up in your very best, take her to a fine restaurant, one of her choosing, and tell her to get nicely dressed with the best she's got to wear and you're going to take her to this restaurant and let her order anything she wants to order. I think that if you people go to this restaurant, have a couple of drinks, eat a nice dinner, you may start something. You may actually get to like each other and he may even take you out some more on some other occasions. This way we can avoid this terrible situation of him being charged with something very serious and for which he could very well be sent to jail for three and one-half to five years. Now, I don't really think you want that. So, how about it? Off to a nice dinner, a nice evening of fun and enjoyment, and then come back here and tell me you don't want to prosecute this case. You don't think it's necessary. I think that would be a nice way to settle this situation; and, by the way, next Sunday, take this young lady fishing." Next case.

Case Fourteen
Swimming in Town Reservoir

I was in my office this hot afternoon, I believe it was on a Wednesday or Thursday, when I got a call from the Police Sergeant that he had an unusual case there and that I should come over and see if I could resolve it. He seemed he really didn't know how to handle it. He said, "Judge, I'm sure you'll figure out some way to take care of the situation."

Well, I went over to the court house and there were seven youngsters who I was told had been picked up for swimming in the village reservoir; the reservoir that supplies drinking water for the people of the village as well as water for other means. I looked at the kids and said, "Is this a fact? Were you swimming in the village reservoir that supplies drinking water in the village as well as water for cooking and other things?" They all admitted that they had been doing so. I thought, "This is pretty serious on two counts. One, they were swimming in the water that people were drinking and secondly there was a very grave danger involved here." So, I said, "Alright, Saturday afternoon 2:00 o'clock is generally the day and the time I set aside to dispose of these juvenile delinquency cases and that's what this is. You are all under age and so you'll all have to be treated as juvenile delinquents. Let's see what happens Saturday when you're here. In the meantime I want your parents here with you." I turned to the police Sergeant and said, "You make sure that those parents are all notified that the judge wants them here on Saturday afternoon at 2:00 o'clock and I don't want anybody missing. And if anybody says they can't make it, or won't make it, you tell them that the judge will issue a warrant." Sergeant said, "For what?" I said, "I'll figure it out, but for the time being you tell them I will charge whoever fails to appear or tells you they won't appear, I will charge them with neglect of his children or his child. It may not hold up in court, but it will be enough to get him over here Saturday."

Well, the case--it's really not a case, it's really a hearing--before we met on Saturday at 2:00 o'clock, I called the Superintendent of the Utility, a Mr. Norton. I said, "Mr. Norton, I want you to come to the court on

Saturday at 2:00 o'clock in the afternoon and to bring with you a fruit jar full of water that I want you to present, to bring with you, to the court house." He said, "Why is that, what's with the water?" I said, "You'll see when you get to the court house why I want you to come here with this jar of water."

So, we started, I reviewed the facts, told the parents that I was very upset about what had happened. I said these youngsters certainly could be charged with trespassing. There were signs all over the place, all around the fence indicating that trespassers will be prosecuted and I said, "But, I don't feel like having these kids obtain a record of some kind that will be with them all their lives. I hope we can resolve this in a manner that will satisfy everybody. First, I want to tell you people that your kids were up there swimming in the reservoir because it was a hot summer day and I think it behooves you to tell the Village Fathers, (your elected officials), to get busy and build a swimming pool so these kids don't have to swim in the reservoir. They can swim in their own swimming pool which is made for that purpose.

"Now, you kids you certainly knew better than to go into that reservoir area, take off your clothes and go swimming. I am told you were all swimming without any clothes on." They nodded their heads. "OK", I said,

"Mr. Norton, will you step forward, please? Hand each one of these kids one of these paper cups." I had seven paper cups on my bench and I asked him to distribute them to each kid. I said, "Into each one of these cups, pour some of that water from the fruit jar you got." He did so, and he stepped back. I said, "Let it be known this water that's in your cup that came from Mr. Norton's fruit jar was taken from his bath this morning. In other words, that water is water from which he had taken a bath, is similar to your situation. You kids swam in the reservoir and that was the area, that was the place you shouldn't be because that reservoir famishes drinking water, cooking water, and for other means to the people of Solvay. So now, I'm going to have you see what it means or how it feels to be drinking water where someone has taken a bath and that's what you were doing. Go right ahead and drink the water in your cup." Well, not a single one of those kids put that cup to their lips. They said, "Judge, please do anything you want to us but please don't make me drink this water." I said, "What's the matter, that's bath water, the water that Village of Solvay residents will be drinking after you were swimming in the reservoir. It's like bath water. They're going to have to drink that water so why shouldn't you have to drink some water likewise?"

Well, I didn't make them drink that water. I knew I had made my point and I knew that these kids realized that it was wrong for them to be swimming in the reservoir--swimming in the water that was used by the people to drink and cook and for other uses.

I said, "I'm going to adjourn this case and think of some way, some how to probably punish you for what you did. But, I want to remind you the notation concerning these cases will only appear in my notebook. They will not appear as an official record of any juvenile violation. I don't want you kids to have this on your record for the rest of your lives but remember, much of this depends on whether or not you behave yourself from now on. If you get into trouble again, if you violate the law again, if you do what you're not supposed to do, then I'll just enter this charge, the disposition and your admission of guilt in the full, official book. In the meantime, you may be assured that this will not appear as an official record. You can tell anybody, anytime, anywhere, filling out any form--Armed Services or if you seek a job with Civil Service or if you fill out any form for any position, that you've never been charged with any violation. But that record, and that treatment remains solely in your hands. You must not get into trouble again. OK.

"Here is your punishment. I want Mr. Norton to tell you kids what needs to be done to make that reservoir neat, clean and better looking. He will take you up on a given day. You're going to mow the lawn up there, or whatever it is, trim whatever hedges there are up there, rake the leaves that are around, fill those little holes that are under the fence so no animals can get in there, and repaint the fence all over. After you have done that and he reports to me, you'll have your cases dismissed.

Parents, take heed. Get after our forefathers, get after the people who run this village, tell them to get that swimming pool so that our kids can enjoy the benefit of swimming in the summer time in a nice, cool, refreshing pool so they won't have to think about jumping into the reservoir. OK, everybody dismissed."

Case Fifteen
Juvenile Truant

This next case involves another juvenile delinquent. This defendant who was, I believe, nine or ten years of age was constantly skipping school. In New York State until you're fifteen years of age you have to be in school every day. But, this boy didn't pay much attention to the law because he had not only skipped school frequently, he had also done a little thievery-not big, but small thievery. I was at a loss as to how to handle this boy and I felt a little sorry for him because his father was in the sanitarium and so his mother really had a tough time trying to raise this boy.

Of course, he was big for his age and the poor mother was beside herself. She said she tried to get him up in the morning, she said she sent him off to school but she had no way of making sure he got there. He just would leave the house after he had his breakfast, then go roaming around the streets and skipping school.

I kind of thought maybe, just maybe, if he had a little more spending money in his pocket he wouldn't be doing so much stealing and not only that, it would kind of keep him busy because he would have something to do every afternoon after he got out of school. Of course on Saturdays he could go around and collect on his route. I knew the distribution Director of the Syracuse-Herald Journal. I had some other affairs with him and we knew each other. I asked him to, please, whenever he found an opening in a paper route to let me know because I would like for him to give it to this boy. He said, "Judge, we're in luck. The boy that has the route, by the way which includes you on the route, is going to quit this Saturday after he makes his collections. So starting Monday, I need a new boy to take care of this route. Tell the boy to be down at the comer of Orchard Row and Milton Avenue at 2:00 o'clock Monday afternoon and I'll tell him what it's all about and hire him.

I sent for the boy, told him what had happened. He seemed agreeable. He said he would go down to the corner and take up the route. Well, I thought maybe I had our problem solved but it didn't turn out that way. Two weeks after he had been on the route, the police sergeant called me and said, "You know that boy of yours that you took such an interest in, he's been in a little trouble again. You'd better come over here. I've got him over here and I want you to handle this because I don't know what to do." I said, "OK, keep him there and I'll be over." When I got there, the sergeant said, "Your boy here has stolen two bicycles. Two women on his route called to say their bicycles had been stolen from their garage and we presumed that it could have probably been your boy here, Robert. (Name fictitious.) So, we picked Robert up, brought him over here and said, "What do you say?" He admitted he had stolen the bicycles; he said he needed a bike because it was so hard carrying all those papers on the route he needed a bicycle so the bicycle would help him carry them and it wouldn't be such a load. Sergeant asked him about the second bike and he said, "I had the second bike so in case something happened to the first bike I got the second one to take its place." I said to Robert, "Is this true?" He said, "Yes, your honor, that's about it. I didn't mean to steal the bicycle, I just wanted to use it on my route and when I got through the route, if I ever finished, I'd give them back." "No", I said, "Robert, that's not possible. If you took those bicycles out of those people's garage attempting to use them for yourself, you stole the bikes. I'm terribly disappointed."

Then the sergeant turned to me and he said, "That's not all your honor" and he reached in his drawer and pulled out three golf balls. He said, "These golf balls, your honor, got your name on them." I took the golf balls from the sergeant, looked at them and sure enough by name, Judge Salvetti, is on these three golf balls. I turned to Robert and said, "What are you going to say to this?" He said, "Judge, I didn't know your name was on those golf balls." It appears at the time that he felt if my name hadn't been on the golf balls it would have been alright to steal the balls.

It turned out that this was about as far as I intended to go with this boy. He was, I think, incorrigible, so I sent him to the Elmira Reform School. The boys when they are sent there are sent for indefinite terms. You see, the director makes the determination so we don't have to have any fixed terms for these kids who are juveniles. He determines whether they have reached a point where they can be released and sent out into the world again and probably behave themselves.

So, I sent him to the Elmira Reform School for the, so called, indefinite term despite his mother's pleading that I not do so. But, I told her, "I have got to do this because Robert here is going to get into serious trouble if I don't do something somehow to make him understand that these things he does are all wrong."

145

Case Sixteen
Juvenile Becomes Air Force Lieutenant

The next juvenile case that I want to report on had a little more pleasant, satisfactory result. It seems this young lad who was at the time about 16 years old, and he too had been skipping school left and right so I had him brought before me the last time that he skipped school and I said to him, "John, (name fictitious) I can't send you back home and expect you to behave yourself. What the heck's going on here? Why are you skipping school? There's nothing going on up there. The teachers aren't mean to you, the principal is not mean to you. Why don't you finish school, you're sixteen years old, you've got one more year to go and then you can go out into the world and do as you please?"

He said, "Your honor, I don't know whether this makes any difference or not, but I'm not happy where I am. You see, my mother gave birth to me out of wedlock and she left me here with my grandmother to raise. Now I very rarely see my own mother because she was working and, of course, going off from time to time enjoying herself and ignoring me completely. It wasn't too bad being raised by a grandmother except that she was fairly young and she had two kids that were younger than me, a girl and a boy, who were my uncle and aunt. Pretty much my grandmother was occupied raising her own kids and spent very little time with me. I'm very unhappy and I don't know, maybe that's why I skip school." So, I said, "I'll tell you what. You come here tomorrow morning and I'll see what I can do about your problem."

He did. I called the school and talked to one of his teachers. In fact, it was a math teacher. She told me that this lad had an IQ of 140. Mind you, he had an IQ of 140. She also told me that he shows up in the math class maybe once or twice a week. But when he takes the exam, he gets a 95 or 96 every time. She said, "I don't know how he does it. He hardly comes to class to get instruction, but when he takes the exam he gets one of the top grades." I thanked the teacher for her wonderful cooperation and her information.

The next morning I said to the young lad, "I have made arrangements to send you to St. Anthony's Military Academy in Albany. I want you to go there. You will be in the Institution until you finish high school. You will be there, actually you won't be able to get out, because you will be there living and doing all the things you're supposed to do at the Academy. So, this is the best I can do but I'm getting you out of that horrible situation that you're in down there with your grandmother and your uncle and aunt who are younger than you. But you'll like it there--I'm sure you'll like it there. You'll be with a number of boys who have been in some trouble, of course, but not serious matters. You'll certainly enjoy the teachers and the fact that you're away and pretty much on your own. I understand that you have a very high Intelligence Quotient, and I think you'll do very well in the school there. So, keep me in touch, let me know what happens. I would like to know--because I certainly want to know whether or not it works out alright.

I'd like to say that about two or three years later this young lad came into my courtroom in full regalia, dressed in an Army uniform with Lieutenant bars on his shoulders. He walked up to the bench and said, "Judge, do you know who I am?" I said, "Really you look familiar, but I just can't place you. You know I do see an awful lot of people here. I'm sorry but I just can't place you right now." He said, "I'm the boy you sent to St. Anthony's Academy in Albany." "Oh," I said, "now I remember. Well, it looks to me like you're doing alright." "Yes, your honor" he said, "and I have you to thank for it. I'm now a Lieutenant in the U. S. Air Force and I prepared for same by the work I did at St. Anthony's Academy which is a military academy. You know, I knew that this was my last chance to succeed and I behaved myself, did what I was supposed to, graduated with honors, got myself into the Army Air Corps and earned my wings. I wanted you to know that, even though I didn't keep in touch with you while I was there--really I was too busy--but I want you to know things are fine, things are going along okay and thanks again."

Boy, did I feel good about that. I couldn't wait to tell my wife what happened. You see once in awhile; well, for the most part, my job brings some pleasure and joy to me and this was one of those occasions I have to admit.

Case Seventeen
Street Lights and BB Guns

Three boys, who lived over in what we always called the Draper Tract, one night with a BB Gun they went up and down the street and shot out all of the street lights. It was a street about four blocks long and things were pretty, pretty bad there because people were getting home late; especially girls and ladies getting home late, got off the bus down at the corner and had to walk the whole length of that street in darkness. And that wasn't good. As a matter of fact, that was why the lights were put up to make sure that the street was lighted and the women didn't have to fear somebody grabbing them from behind--maybe raping them.

At any rate, the police found out who shot the lights out, brought them over to my court and said, "Here you are Judge, here are the culprits who shot out those street lights." I thanked the sergeant, turned to the kids and said, "I want to see you at 2:00 o'clock Saturday afternoon and I want your parents with you. I turned to the sergeant and said, "Be sure the parents are notified that they are to be here Saturday afternoon with these kids. I want to see them and I want to talk to them and I want them to know that their children are in deep trouble."

I turned to Mr. Norton again and said, "Mr. Norton, I have a little job for you. I think you can help me. I want you to let me know how much the four bulbs cost that were replaced up there and how much time your men had to spend and figure out from the time they spent on replacement what they earned in the way of wages that the village had to pay. I want a total figure, if you can make it possible for me to understand the true cost of replacing those street lights." He said he would do so, and by the time Saturday rolled around he had all the figures and had submitted them to me.

So, Saturday when the case was scheduled again, parents were all present, kids were present; I turned to the kids and I said, "Who owned the BB gun?" One of the kids raised his hand. I said, "I'm not going to punish him any more man the others because if the others did some shooting too, you're all equally guilty. But I just want to know who owned the BB Gun so I can talk to the parents of that boy. When they buy a BB Gun for a child, they had better let him know exactly what they expect him to use it for."

The punishment was the amount Mr. Norton figured out to be the cost of replacemtn of the lights, bulbs and labor. I gave the kids a three month adjournment to raise the money to pay for the damages.

Case Eighteen
School Breakin

This case involved kids who broke into the high school, went in to the science lab and did about $2,000 worth of damage. They smashed the experiments that were in effect, they smeared chemicals all over the place. As I say, they did about $2,000 worth of damage and when they came before me, of course, I told them to appear Saturday afternoon at 2:00 o'clock Saturday afternoon with their parents.

When we convened again Saturday afternoon at 2:00 o'clock, I decided to take each one of these kids into my office and question then individually to see if I could get to the bottom of this. I took the first one into the office, sat him down and asked him the following questions: "Were you mad at somebody in the school, a teacher, some other employee?" "No." "Were you mad at the principal?" "No." "Were you mad at the superintendent." "No." "Were you mad at anybody connected with the school to cause you to want to get back at them or get some revenge by doing this damage?" "No." "Well, then tell me, why in heaven's name did you go into this school and do all that damage?" His answer, "I don't know." Well, that was about it with him.

I called the other boy in and asked him the same questions--whether he was mad about anybody, mad about the teacher, mad about the school, mad about his parents, angry about anything. He said, "No" to all the questions. Then I asked him finally, "Then why did you do this? Why did you go in there and do all this damage?" His answer, "I don't know."

Well, I dismissed him, called the last one in, went through the same rigamarole, asked the same questions, got the same answers and finally asked him. "Why did you do this?" His answer, "I don't know." This was a real dilemma for me. I had three boys that I had to handle who couldn't give me any excuse whatsoever as to why they went into that school, went into the lab room and did all that damage. I turned to the parents and I said to them, "Have you any answer to the question why they went in there and did all that damage?" The parents, all six of them said they had no idea, they were shocked that their boys had done so and they couldn't understand why they had gone in there and done all the damage.

So, I turned to them and said, "Well, what do you think I ought to do. I know that damage has to be repaid, the school and the tax payers aren't going to pay for all that repairing that has to be done. These kids somehow are going to have to pay for that damage. Or, if they don't, certainly you people, parents of these kids will have to do it. Otherwise, I'll have to be pretty harsh in my treatment in reference to this particular case. I don't want to take these boys away from you and send them to Elmira if I can help it; especially since I have found from the records that they have not committed any crimes at all, minor or otherwise. So I'm inclined to feel that perhaps on this occasion we could come to a different solution other than removing them from their homes and sending them to the Elmira Reform School. I'm at a loss at this time, right now, to figure out how to punish these boys for what they did. I wish you could help me, but I know you can't. So here's what Fm going to do. I'm gooint to adjourn this case for three months. The total bill, the repair bill, for the damages they did will be figured out and submitted to you parents by the principal. And, these kids somehow between now and three months from now are going to have to do jobs, run errands, maybe get a paper route, mow lawns, do little handy work things around the houses and around the neighborhood; but they are going to have to work and raise the money to pay these damages. So, I'm adjourning these cases until three months from today at which time I hope and pray, really, that these boys raise the money to defray the cost of repairing the damage they did in the school. Okay, case adjourned. Next Case"

Case Nineteen
Pool Damage

I can't believe it. It wasn't too long after I had that case involving the kids in the school house damage that the police brought before me four boys who had damaged the bath house and some of the pool that was located in the playground which was provided by the village just shortly before the event.

I went through the same motion with these boys, took each one of them separately into my office and asked them the questions--were they mad at somebody? did somebody like the director of parks or life savers that were at the parks, did they do something that caused you to feel angry, seek revenge? Were you at all upset about whatever was going on in the park program? Every question that I asked, they came up with a "No."

And then I asked the big questions, "Then tell me why you did it?" The answer was, "I don't know."

I took all four of those boys into my office, individually, one at a time and asked them the same question. They all answered that they were not mad at anybody, they weren't upset about anything and they all answered that they just didn't know why they did the damage. Well, I turned to the parents in this case too and said, "There you are, there you have it. I don't know what to do about this. I certainly don't want to take these kids away from their family, away from you parents, send them to Elmira Reform School, especially since they have never committed any other crimes-minor or otherwise. But I can't let them go free; I can't let them go unpunished. I'm really at a loss as to what to do. I don't think you parents can give me any help because- well, they're your kids. But somehow you should show some responsibility for what went on. These kids out of nowhere decided to damage the swimming pool and the bath house--two facilities which were primarily built for them to enjoy as well as other kids in the area and here they go, break in at night and do about $1,500 worth of damage.

I really don't know what goes on in the minds of these kids. I really can't figure out whatever possessed them to think they could do this damage and get away with it. And I cannot figure out, in any way, why they would possibly do this kind of damage to a public facility." At any rate, I adjourned the case for a week to give myself some time to think about it. In the meantime I contacted the Chief Psychiatrist at the New York State Psychiatric Hospital. I told him what my problem was and I asked him for some help. I told him that every one of these kids, both in the school house case and this one involving the bath house, all answered by saying, "I don't know, I don't know." I said, "Doctor, I gathered from my interviews with these kids that they really didn't have a sound excuse or a good reason for doing the damage, except, I don't know, maybe they got some pleasure out of doing what they did. I've come to you, and I ask you for help so that I can determine how I can best handle these cases, how much or what kind of punishment I should mete out, or, in other words, I'm asking you to help me figure out how best I can handle these cases both from the point of view of punishing them because they've done wrong and also from the point of view of not creating for them a criminal record that will live with them for the rest of their life. I just hate to think that these young boys here in their youth will be doing certain things that would follow them for life. That, alone, would be the greatest amount of punishment--going through life with a record indicating that they are very bad boys." The doctor said, I think I'd like to talk to the boys, at least one or two of them because they all seem to be in the same boat. When can I do so?" I said, "Anytime you say Doctor, I'll have them there. They're on summer vacation and they can appear anytime, any day that you wish."

We set a day, 2:00 o'clock in the afternoon. I told the parents to be there with the boys that I was going to have someone talk to the boys and find out what was in their minds--find out why they did the damage, what possessed them to do the things they did; especially, since I'm sure they knew, without question, that what they were doing was wrong and I don't doubt for a moment that they don't really believe that they should go without punishment of some kind.

The doctor interviewed two of the boys who had damaged the bath house and then he said, "I'll send you my report as soon as I get back to the office and maybe I've been some help, I don't know." I thanked the doctor and told him that if he had a bill or had to be paid for his services to send a bill to the Village Clerk's office and he would be reimbursed. He said, "No, I'm doing this on my own. I want to help. I understand your dilemma and I understand your problem and I understand that you're trying to do the best you can to save the boys from a life of crime and at the same time figure out some way of punishing what they have done."

He sent me the report shortly thereafter and said, in effect, "I got the same answer you did and, believe me, they really had no purpose, no excuse, no reason for doing the damage. When they said they didn't know, they were telling you the truth. I did conclude, however, that this is just a possible answer to the problem. I don't have a complete basic fundamental one and that is that I think perhaps they were doing this to get some attention from their parents. I think they thought that if they did this damage and made a noise, created a problem, their parents would be notified, their parents would have to do something about it and their parents would certainly have to give some attention to what went on. I think," said the doctor, "that's about as close as I can come to coming up with an answer."

On the adjourned date, I had the four boys and their parents in the court room. We try to hold these cases, of course, with the jury out, free of any newspaper people or busy bodies--they're supposed to be held in a manner that's as close to being private as possible and I did just that. I told them what the psychiatrist had said and I told the parents that they had better spend more time and give more attention to these kids because the psychiatrist seemed to think that they needed more attention and they needed for you people to be a little more concerned about what the kids were doing, where they were going and how they were spending their spare time.

So I said, "Well, here is my punishment. I'm turning you boys over to the Director of Parks and for the rest of the summer you're going to work for him and with him in the park program. You're going to be mowing lawns, cutting grass, trimming shrubbery, raking up the ball parks, you're going to be painting, you're going to be doing all the things the park people do to keep and maintain the parks for the summer. You're going to have to show up every morning with Mr. Jones (name fictitious) and be ready to work eight hours a day all the rest of the summer until enough money is accumulated by figuring out what your wages would be, at the minimum wage of course, and that money which is going to be paid to you for the work you did, will be used to redo the damage. So that's your penalty. You must do this and if you don't, the Director will tell me who, which one of you, or if all of you failed to perform and then you'll be back here again this fall for further punishment for your wrongdoing. Case adjourned."

Case Twenty
Pinball Machine Robbery

As luck would have it, this case involved a juvenile delinquency crime and here I was really stuck with a very serious violation. Four boys broke into this tavern and stole the nickels out of the pinball machine. The police didn't have much trouble apprehending them because they had gone to a grocery store, and the police had alerted all the grocers in the area. They had gone to the grocery store and wanted to exchange this $15 worth of nickels into dollar bills. The grocer, of course, notified the police, the police came down, picked them up and they were brought up in front of me.

Mind you, they were juvenile delinquents, but they committed a burglary! How does one handle a crime that serious when it's committed by a juvenile and the charge has to be treated accordingly. Well, I had them appear after the arraignment on Saturday afternoon. Again, I arranged to have their parents present. I don't discuss any cases or problems with the juvenile delinquents themselves without having the parents present because I feel they should know what's going on, what's happening, what did happen, and help me straighten these kids out.

Now, what do you do about somebody, even if they're juveniles, who break into a tavern and steal nickels out of the pinball machine? I, again, found out they had never done anything wrong before--this was their first offense. I felt that if they didn't do anything wrong again for the rest of their lives, they would probably learn from this experience not to do anything wrong again. But it depended on me to make sure that I handled the case properly to be sure that the lesson comes across.

I, again, did not want to separate them from their family, send them to Elmira Reform School. I was hopeful that I could teach them or encourage them or help them stay straight. So, again, I took them all, one by one, into my office and asked them the questions: "Mad at anybody? Don't have enough money to spend for yourself? Have a fight with your father over an allowance?" "No", No," "Mad at the man who owned the tavern?" "No." "Well, if you didn't need the money, you got an allowance, you weren't mad at anybody, why did you do what you did?" The same answer, "I don't know."

It was amazing to me that all these kids who got into trouble had one answer for why they did the things that they did and it was always, "I don't know." The other boy that I talked to, asked the same questions, came up with the same answer. Also replied when I asked about can you tell me why he did what he did, and I even said on this occasion "Please tell me why you did what you did because this can help me not only in your case but it can help me decide future cases. Give me some inkling as to how I should handle these cases. These are not ordinary criminal cases but you know I have to treat you as juvenile delinquents. I have to make sure that my treatment is such that you don't continue to go on committing crimes. I have to make sure that what I do here with you and for you will always prevent you from doing the same thing again or at least getting involved in some criminal activity again. So, please give me an answer, why did you break in and steal the nickels knowing it was wrong and certainly expecting that maybe you'd be caught and brought before me for punishment."

I adjourned the case for a week, told the parents to be there also and the kids to appear in court.

Saturday afternoons I close the courtroom for just juveniles, no grownups, no newspaper reporters, no people busybodies, nobody at all, just the participants themselves. In this case, involving the nickels that were stolen, I asked the owner of the tavern to also appear on Saturday at 2:00 o'clock so I could get his view on a number of things: What really happened, how much damage was done by breaking into the pinball machine or if there was any other damage, or any other thefts, and I really thought perhaps I could get some advice from him as to how he thought I should handle the case.

Well, the Saturday that we appeared didn't bear much results. The tavern keeper wanted the kids punished severely. He was very mad, very angry. He said, "They ought to be sent away, they're bad boys, they're criminals and if I were to do my duty I'd send them off to Elmira Reform School where they belong." I, of course, didn't quite agree with him. I didn't think they were really criminals. I didn't think they were to be that severely punished. But I knew somehow, someway I had to do something to show them that they couldn't get away with theft. I turned to the tavern keeper and I said, "Tell me, are there any odd jobs around your place of business: Painting scrubbing floors, scrubbing the booths, scrubbing the bar, scrubbing the bathroom floor, cleaning up the bathroom facilities, anything you've got that need attention?" He said, "Yes, there are always some things that need attention, why are you asking me?" I said, "I'm asking you because I think I'm going to make sure that these kids appear and report to you and do that work as part of the punishment, not the total punishment, but as part of the punishment for what they did." "Well," he said "that's okay with me, but I still think you ought to send them to Elmira Reform School. They're nothing but criminals, they're thieves, and they should be punished severely and you as the judge ought to do your job and send them off to jail." "Well," I said "Mr. Jones, (name fictitious) it's not that easy. I keep thinking possibly one of these boys could have been your son. How would you feel if one of them was your son and another tavern was involved? And that tavern keeper came and wanted your son sent to Elmira Reform School, that he be treated as a criminal, that he be given no leniency, no consideration at all. I don't think you'd be here saying, 'Send him to jail', so, you see, I have to consider all of the factors. They've never been in trouble before, this is their first offense, they seem to be good boys, they seem to come from nice families; I have to be careful how I handle the case because if I don't do what's right they could carry this stigma against themselves on their record for the rest of their lives. That alone could possibly lead to further violations. You know, they could say, 'So I've got a black mark against me, so I've got a stigma here that will remain with me for the rest of my life, so what difference does it make. I can't get rid of it and I'm always going to be treated as though I'm a criminal even though I did this when I was young, inexperienced and didn't know any better.' So you see, Mr. Jones, it's not that easy being a judge. He has all these factors to consider and I intend to do so here. So please be patient and understanding and recognize that my role is not that simple. I just can't take these kids and say, 'You're guilty, you robbed, off you go', away from home to Elmira Reform School where I'm pretty sure they learn a lot more about crime than they can from the streets of Solvay."

I did that. I ordered these kids to report to the tavern keeper and to do any kind of job, cleanups, spittoon, he directed.

Case Twenty One
Neighbor Keeps Ball

I had another case involving kids. It seems like I had my share of juvenile delinquency cases all the while I was serving on the bench. At any rate, these kids were in the habit of playing out in the street: Football, hockey, whatever and along the street this man, Mr. Jones (name fictitious), had a large fence surrounding about four or five building lots that he used for gardening. He planted tomatoes, potatoes, corn, all sorts of crops and the kids when they were playing out in the street from time to time would cause their football to go over the fence and they would just climb over the fence and retract it.

Well, the man that owned that property and actually had that garden wasn't very happy about the fact that they were running around trampling on his tomato plants and so forth. So he worked out a deal with the police and the police worked out with the kids in the neighborhood --they agreed that if a ball, baseball, softball, football or any other ball went over into his garden, they would not climb the fence and go over and retrieve it. They would just stand by and when he came over to work in his garden they'd tell him about it and then he would supposedly give it back to them.

It so happened they were playing one day and the ball went over the fence. They were abiding by the agreement they had made. They didn't climb the fence and didn't try to retrieve it. They just got another ball or played some other game and when Mr. Jones came to the garden to work in his garden they told him the football was there, would he please throw it over the fence back to them. He looked at the kids and said, "Ah, ha. I've got your football and I'm not gonna give it back to you because anytime the ball comes over here sometimes it hits a plant and sometimes it doesn't but sometimes when it hits a plant it just gives me more trouble so I'm not gonna give you the ball." One of the kids turned to him and said, "But Mr. Jones, we made an agreement. We would not climb the fence and retrieve the ball. We would stand by and wait 'til you came down here," (he lived a little way away from the lots,) "and that you in turn would throw the ball back to us so that we could continue to play and you're not doing that." He said, "No, and I don't intend to."

So one of the young boys came over to the police station and said he wanted to see the judge. I said, "Okay." He came into the office and told me the whole story. I said, "Is that the way it happened? He kept your football? Wouldn't give it back to you?" "That's right." Well you know footballs were not cheap, even then. They cost three or four dollars and three or four dollars was pretty hard to come by. So I sent the patrolman over to see Mr. Jones and to tell him that he should give that football to the kids and live up to the agreement they had made as long as the kids stayed out of his garden and he told the policeman, "I'm not going to give them that football because they'll be playing around again and next thing I know it'll go over the fence and we'll be right back where we started from--their asking for me to return the football and here I am trying to raise some crops and the kids are out there fooling around. They don't have any business playing out there in the street anyway." The patrolman said, "Okay, I'm gonna report that back to the judge." He came back and reported to me. He said he's not gonna return the football and he said, "You kids had no business playing out there in the street anyway." I said, "That's what he said?" "Yes." "Okay", I said to the patrolman, "Go find that youngster over there on Worth Avenue. He's probably over there somewhere. Find out who he is, bring him over here, I want to talk to him."

An hour or so later the policeman brought the boy over. The boy told me the same story and I said to him, "Listen, you lived up to your agreement, you did what you were supposed to and Mr. Jones didn't. So, you're no longer bound by any agreement that was formerly made. If your football goes over into his garden, go and retrieve it. We'll teach him that an agreement is something you're supposed to live by and not take advantage of." The youngster was about 12 or 13 years old said, "Thank you Judge, thank you very much. We'll do what you say."

Case Twenty Two
Gambling

One morning I was holding court and it seemed the police had given a summons to a Mr. Smith (name fictitious) who was being charged with running a gambling establishment in the Village which, of course, was against the law.

I read the charge to the defendant, told him she had a right to plead guilty or not guilty, he had a right to have the matter in the case adjourned, given an opportunity to hire and attorney or to think about it. At any rate, we could adjourn the case at his convenience, to prepare for trial or to do whatever he thought he might want to do.

He said, "Your honor, I don't see anybody here from the Reynolds and Company. Why am I here being charged with running a gambling establishment and there's nobody here from the Reynolds and Company, the brokerage firm." I looked at the defendant and said, "What's that got to do with this case? What's the Reynolds Company got to do with this case--that's a brokerage firm licensed by the State of New York? People go in there buy and sell stocks, they sit around and watch to see what the stock market's doing. How does that compare with what you were doing. You were running a gambling establishment. You had men in your place of business watching the board to see what teams were going to win at baseball or whatever else was the sport that was going on--racing. How does running a brokerage firm compare with your running a gambling institution where the people are betting on races, the outcome of football games, baseball games, basketball and so forth?" He said, "Well your honor, have you ever been at one of those brokerage firms offices?" I said, "Yes, I've been in there on occasion-dabble a little bit in the stock market--not much, but I've been in there and seen what goes on." He said, "Well, had you noticed that the men all sitting there are betting on whether the stock goes up or whether the stock goes down, that they're betting to see where they're going to put their money. If they think that the stock is gonna go down, they sell it or do what you call a put and call. If they think the stock is going up, they're gambling that it might go up so they buy the stock hoping it goes up three or four points, then they sell it. They make three or four points. That, to me, is gambling."

I sat back for a few moments. I said, "You know, there's a lot to what you say. I remember when I was interested somewhat in the stock market--not much, but at any rate I was sorta betting that the stock market would rise. I know there were people in that room, that brokerage firm room, who were also what you call selling short or long, I forget which. But anyway selling the stock with the idea that it was going to go down and whoever bought it from them would have to buy it at the price they were selling it and they would save money. Yes, I would have to say that the people who deal in the stock market are really gambling that the stock will either go up or it will go down. I think you have a point. But I'm not in a position to rule on such a situation.

"I don't know of any incident in which the people at the Reynolds Brokerage Firm were ever charged with gambling, but that's what they're doing. I don't know if that's very much different from what you're doing. People are paying that a certain horse would win the race or a certain team would win the game. I don't like what I'm hearing. So I'll tell you what I'm going to do. If you will promise me to close your shop, close your gambling joint and stop what you're doing, and have no more gambling going on such as it is, by you in this Village. I'm going to adjourn this case for a month and if you close shop, stop the gambling, give up what you're doing and have no more of this betting going on anywhere in the Village, I might be inclined to dismiss this charge against you based on all the facts that I'm party to right now. See you in one month from today."

Case Twenty Three
Prostitution

Another case that bears my talking about involved a matter of prostitution. Now I know that prostitution is one of the oldest professions in history and that it's pretty hard to stop it. But the law's the law and my job is to see to it that people who violate the law are in some way punished, or at least made to understand that they are not to continue with the practice.

This morning a girl appeared in court but she had with her an attorney. I thought that odd, but he came forth and said, "Your honor, I represent Mary Jones (name fictitious) in this prostitution charge and I see that we're the only case here in front of you this morning and I wonder why the police made it their business to just arrest my client and nobody else? I don't see why she should be made the scapegoat or she should be the one who should be punished for engaging in this life of prostitution when others who are doing the same thing go scott free, don't even get prosecuted." I said, "Come now, you're not trying to tell me that the police just picked this one defendant out of the group, charged her with this crime, give her a summons directing her to appear before me and didn't do anything about the rest of them?" "Well," he said "It's not quite exactly that way, but Judge up there in the James Street Apartments prostitution goes on every day and nothing is done about it."

I said, "What has the James Street Apartments got to do with this case?"

He said, "Well, most of those girls up there are kept women--wealthy executives,--businessmen have these girls ensconced in those apartments up there. They pay their rent, they pay for the apartments, they furnish them with money for food, they buy them fancy clothes, fancy jewelry, and treat them like queens. And the only thing those girls can give those executives in return for all of that largess is sex. Now that is strictly prostitution. They're being paid for sex. They may not be standing on the street corner, they may not be in some barroom picking up trade, but they're just as guilty as my client selling what they got for the nice apartment, clothing, jewelry, good times, dinners and so forth. That, to me, is the same as paying a prostitute who picks up ten bucks or fifteen bucks for peddling her wares."

I stopped and thought for a moment, how right this lawyer was. There isn't any question, if these women were kept, provided with all these fancy things, and they're giving these executives sex in return, they're just as much a prostitute as this defendant in front of me. But, I thought, am I going to be able to make a decision here that will affect this whole situation? Am I going to stop that from going on in the James Street Apartments? Are the people in this community going to be concerned about my stopping that happening up there? They know it as well as I do. They don't seem to be disturbed. I guess because it's up on a higher level. They don't seem to be worried about what is happening. I guess because it's not open and above-board such as we see here with just normal, everyday prostitution. But I said, "Counselor, you make a point--it disturbs me no end that I should be expected to punish this defendant who is doing nothing differently than those girls up there in the James Street Apartments who are selling what they get for the goodies that they get in return. Let me adjourn this case for a week. Give me a chance to think it over, think of what you just told me. In the meantime, please, no more such activity on your part. I don't want you picked up again and brought in here again and charged with prostitution. Please, I want you to make sure that you behave yourself and you don't appear before me for any crime.

And what despairs me too, also, is the fact, counselor, that anytime I have a case of this nature, it's always the prostitute that's brought here in court to confront me. Nobody ever picks up the pimp, nobody ever charges the pimp, nobody ever charges him or prosecutes him. It's always the girl who is charged with the crime. That's something that rubs me the wrong way. I'd like to see the pimps apprehended and charged with a crime, which they are, and maybe if we made the pimps pay the price, we could cut down on the prostitution, or even eliminate it. But believe me, counselor, we're not going to eliminate prostitution if we continue along the same lines that we're doing now. This is one of the tasks before me which I don't relish I really don't relish handling or presiding over cases of prostitution because I know somehow, I have a gut feeling somehow, that we're never going to truly eliminate it and punishing or fining these girls who find themselves in a position mostly trying to get enough money to get by because they've been kicked out of their house, don't have any money, don't have shelter, no place to sleep and sometimes they turn to prostitution because that's about all they have to turn to. Most of them don't have the education they need to get a good job. Most of them are thrown out of their home because their father is upset that they came home late at night one or two times.

"I have a great deal of sympathy for these women because if you stop to think about it, this business of prostitution is a horrible thing. These women giving their body to strangers. It must be a terribly uncomfortable task. At any rate, let's adjourn this case for a week, come back again, give me time to decide what I should do and, please, young lady don't get involved in anything that would bring you before me again. Stay out of trouble and go to your priest, go to your minister, go to the organizations where they can help. Tell them I sent you, tell them I want you to get help. I want you to be able to find a place to sleep. I want you to be able to get food. I want you to be able to get help with reference to employment. I don't want you to continue in this practice. I'll see you in one week."

Case Twenty Four
Racial Problem

This case is of interest because it deals with a racial problem. The Frasier Jones Company's employees were on strike. Many of the employees were at the gates trying to prevent the strike-breakers from coming into the plant.

The police picked up about seven of them who were charged with malicious mischief. It seems they were spiking the tires of those who were coming in, smashing their headlights, taillights and so forth. The seven appeared with their attorney, who was appointed, of course, or chosen by their Union boss. They all pleaded "not guilty" and I sent the case down for adjournment to try after a fashion and that was it. Except that the next morning another individual was brought in by the police but he was an African/American. He was really black and he was brought before me charged with the same thing, but he was alone with no lawyer. I asked him, "How are you going to plead?" and he said, "I might as well plead 'guilty'". I said, "Wait a minute, I don't like to have anybody in this court room tell me he might as well plead guilty. There's an inference there that somehow you won't get justice here. Tell me about it." What he said was "The Union boss didn't tell the lawyer to represent me too because he feared I might taint the lawsuit somehow, being black, the jury or even the judge might decide that 'well' everybody's guilty, so I don't have a lawyer and I can't afford one. So I think the best thing for me to do is plead 'guilty', take my licking and go on with it." I said, "No such way. You're going to enter a plea of not guilty' and I'm adjourning your case to the same meeting time that the other seven have had their cases adjourned to. In the meantime you tell that Union boss that I said the lawyer representing the other seven is also supposed to represent you. You were all doing the same thing, allegedly guilty of mischief. I don't know whether you were or not, that's for the final decision. But I do know that you are entitled to an attorney and you tell that Union boss that I said you are entitled to have the same representation as the other seven because you're all in the same boat.

And one more thing, if that lawyer says to you when you talk to him or the Union boss says to you, you're not going to do so, you just tell him I'm going to appoint that lawyer to serve you, to represent you pro bono which means he's not going to get paid for representing you. He is going to be appointed by me to represent you because you cannot afford an attorney. Okay, you go your way and show up here with the other seven."

I could see that this case had ramifications of racism and I wasn't going to stand for that in my court--never, never would I stand for an injustice because of race or color creed. Everybody in my court would be treated alike.

Case Twenty Five
Critic's Son Charged

The Chief of Police and I both belonged to the Kiwana's Club which was the Solvay Village Kiwana's Club located in our area and almost invariably at every meeting we'd be harangued by officers of the club because we weren't doing our job. I was accused of being soft on the culprits who were picked up and charged with traffic crimes, speeding and so forth. And the chief, of course, was criticized because he didn't put enough pressure on his policemen to make the number of arrests that should be made.

We took it in stride, and we went along about our business doing just what we usually do. Then one morning this young man came before me charged with drunken driving. As I usually do, I won't accept a plea because the punishment is very severe. If you're found guilty or plead guilty you lose your license for a whole year and your registration if you own a car. That's a long wait and then you have to start all over again by making an appointment, taking a test, doing all the things initially that you would if you were just starting off. I also thought that in some way a fine or punishment or maybe even a suspension of a driver's license for four or five months would have been ample punishment. But I didn't make the law--it's my job to enforce it.

Any way, I told the boy, "Enter a plea of 'not guilty' come here next week, same time, same place and we'll see what we can do about this case. We'll proceed to carry on with a full prosecution or whatever. But in the meantime you contact a good lawyer and have him here to represent you because this case is very serious and you should have the best representation and the best defense possible to make sure that everything has been done right." He thanked me and went off about his business.

The next morning I got a call from his father, John Jones (name fictitious). He was one of those officers at the Kiwana's Club who was always riding me and the Chief for not doing our duty. I thought it funny that he'd want to talk to me about his son's case, but I understood. Things are different when it happens to you or your family. He came in, he sat down and I asked him what

I could do for him. He said, "My son was picked up for drunken driving. He appeared here yesterday and I have learned that if he is found guilty of this charge, he could lose his license for a whole year. He's a commuter. He commutes between our house and the University and he really needs the car to go back and forth and if he loses his license, he has to go back and forth by bus. That's going to be a tough job -- very inconvenient and the schedule will probably not meet with the same schedule that he has in the way of classes." So I said, "Well, what do you want me to do about it? Aren't you one of those people that kept harping about the fact that we weren't tough enough on these violators?" "Yes," he said "I was, but I can see now why it makes a difference if it's somebody in your own family or someone you know quite well. It's not the same as sitting back and telling these people like yourself--do your job, punish these people, stop the crime, stop the speeding, stop the violations. I am pleading with you. I would like to know what I can possibly do to save my boy's license." I said, "Well, I feel pretty much the same as you do. I don't want to see him lose his license either. He hasn't got a record, he hasn't been in trouble before. He hasn't even got a speeding ticket against his name so I understand. He tells me he was at the bash that the fraternity was having at the time and he drank a little too much-that usually he doesn't drink and drive but on this occasion, it was because there was some kind of party celebration at his fraternity at the University, he did indulge just a little bit too much. But, at any rate, I would like to see him save his license. So, I'll tell you what. This case is adjourned for a week. Before he comes back here again on the day of adjournment, I suggest you contact a top criminal lawyer here in the Syracuse area-one who will really represent him completely and fully. The best thing I can tell you is that you have him properly represented by a lawyer who knows about these kind of cases and maybe he'll find some loophole or some little manner or something anyway that'll give him an opportunity to save his license. So you go ahead, hire a good lawyer and be here with your son next week on the adjournment day."

On the adjournment day, with respect to this case, the son, his father and a lawyer--a very well known lawyer, a very highly respected lawyer appeared in my court. He said, "Your honor, I would like to have another week's adjournment to give me an opportunity to look this over, check all the facts, see what I can do to save this boy's license." I said, "Granted, take your time, we're in no hurry. Go ahead and read the record and any help we can give you, please call on us. I'm here to help as well as to punish. I think you know that." He said, "Well, thanks Judge."

They came back a week later and he said, "I think I have a deal. I talked to the Assistant District Attorney handling this case and he said that the percentage that proved to be after the test in the boy's blood stream was only one-thousandth of a percentage--in other words his percentage was .113 and .112 is the line of demarcation. So you can see how close this came to not being a drunken driving charge.

Because of the closeness of the matter, it was not a straight case of drunken driving. No action, nobody got hurt and that's about the facts. "I talked to the Assistant District Attorney" the lawyer said, "and he's agreeable to have you drop the case of drunken driving and have him plead guilty to 'driving impaired'. Of, course, in order to do that we need your consent, the courts'." I said, "I have no objection I can see that possibly the jury may not even convict him of drunken driving. He's a good looking young man, has a nice excuse, sounds plausible, as to why he was drinking a little too much that day. If he pleads guilty to 'driving while impaired', I'll accept that in lieu of dismissing the charge against him for drunken driving. I hope he understands and I'm sure you must have told him that being guilty of driving impaired means he'll lose his license for 30 days. In other words his license and registration are both suspended for 30 days, but only for 30 days after which time he can continue to drive and continue to go about his business just as if nothing happened as far as driving is concerned. But be sure to tell him that if he ever gets caught again driving while intoxicated nobody will be able to help him, I'm sure. He'll suffer the most dire consequences that the law commands. Okay, have him come in. Have him plead guilty to driving impaired and we will dismiss the charge of driving while intoxicated."

I turned to the father and said, "I hope you're satisfied with the results of this case." He said, "Your honor, more than satisfied and I know now what a tough job it is to be a judge and how hard it is to do what you think is right. But I'm grateful and thankful that you're making it possible for my boy to continue after a one-month suspension driving back and forth to college and whatever else he chooses to do as far as driving a car is concerned. You can bet your life, sir, that there'll be no more complaints coming from me or anybody that I can induce to follow suit. Again, thank you very much." I said, "Well, we live and learn, don't we?"

Case Twenty Six
Misunderstood Punishment

I had another case which was unusual, but interesting, and I thought would bear repeating here. This young man came into my court charged with driving while intoxicated. We were commanded by the Commissioner of Vehicular Traffic in the State of New York that whenever anybody is charged with a violation as severe as drunken driving, we had to read him this warning: "Sir, I am advising you that if you plead guilty or if you are found guilty there will be a mandatory revocation of your license including whatever other penalty the court may issue or grant in your case."

I read this warning to the young man, asked him how he pleaded and he said, "I'm guilty, your honor." So I turned to the clerk and I said, "Okay, here's his license, here's his registration, he has pleaded guilty to driving while intoxicated, send them to Albany." That's the routine and that's the practice. The defendant looked at me and he said, "Wait a minute, you're taking my license and registration away. Why are you doing that?" I said, "Young man, I told you at the very beginning that if you pleaded guilty or if you were found guilty of this charge, you would lose your license. I said there would be a mandatory revocation of your license." He looked me straight in the eye and said, "Judge, what's with this mandatory, schmandatory revocation. Why didn't you just say to me 'Sir, if you plead guilty to this charge of driving while intoxicated, I'm gonna take your license and your registration away and send them to Albany and you won't be able to drive for a whole year."

Well, I looked at the young man and I said, "Touche. I can see that you probably didn't understand the warning. And I can also see that if you are told that if you pleaded guilty that your license would be taken away, that's pretty easy to understand. So, I'm going to permit you to withdraw your plea of guilt. I'm going to hold your license and registration because I do that as a matter of practice. You cannot drive while this case is pending except to go to and from work, or to and from your doctor's office, or any other emergency of a similar nature. When the case is over with, depending on the outcome, then you'll either have your license truly revoked or you'll have it returned. But in the meantime remember, if you're picked up any place except a direct to and from your work, to and from your doctor, or to and from an emergency situation, you're driving without an operator's license and that could call for a very severe punishment. So watch out, be careful and don't take the risk. You've got enough trouble ahead of you with this initial charge."

And I also said, "I also recommend that you be back here next week. I'll fix the bail--it won't be too high. But anyway, I'm holding your license so I don't think you're going to run away. But anyway, you come back here next week with your lawyer, tell him your story, explain what happened. Maybe he can help you save your license. Okay, next case."

Case Twenty Seven
Assault Third Degree

This case was sort of unusual in a way, and that's why I'm reporting it. The trial involving a young lad, although I question whether he was guilty of assault, third degree, was arraigned, he appeared with his lawyer and we had the trial.

I listened to the evidence and so did the jury obviously and I couldn't see, for the life of me, how he could escape being charged with the crime and found guilty. But, at any rate, the jury was out for quite awhile, at least a couple of hours, then they came in. The foreman said, "We can't agree your honor. This is really a hung jury." And I said, "What's the problem?" I said, "Do you think if you had a little more time maybe you could convince somebody there who doesn't agree with the majority, maybe we can have a verdict and won't have to try this case over." "No," he said, "your honor I'm pretty sure. We tried very hard, but this lady, he pointed her out, won't budge. She says he is not guilty and she's gonna stand there until hell freezes over.

"We spent another half hour going over the evidence, explaining to her what the consequences would be if we didn't find a verdict, but she was adamant. She would not change her mind, so we can't come out with a unanimous verdict, so you might as well dismiss it."

I thought it odd. I thought the evidence was pretty straight. I thought the evidence was pretty clear, so after the case was over with and the jury was dismissed, I sent for this lady and asked her to come into my chambers with me. I wanted to talk to her. I don't know whether that was correct or not. I really didn't care, but I just wanted to know why she felt so strongly that this boy was innocent and not guilty as charged. Well, she came in, sort of reluctantly, but she sat down and I said, "You don't have to tell me anything. You don't have to tell me what went on, you don't have to tell me why you did what you did, you don't have to tell me anything about this, but I'm curious. I listened to the evidence and I was fairly satisfied that the prosecution was proving beyond a reasonable doubt that this boy was guilty. But it's the jury system and, of course, the verdict has to be unanimous and you have every right in the world to have looked at the evidence differently than the other five. But I'm curious. What was there about this trial? Was there anything about this trial that made you feel so strongly about it?" She said, "Normally I wouldn't tell anybody about it but, your honor, I'm going to tell you because I think you conducted yourself very well. You didn't show any partiality, you ruled on all the rules that came about where there were objections and so forth. I thought you did a good job. I'll tell you what. This testimony was based solely, primarily and largely on the evidence produced here and introduced by police officers. I don't believe police officers. They are a bunch of liars. They'll lie and tell a story and do anything to get a conviction. That's an experience I had with a police officer involving my own son and I vowed that if at any time I was in a position to repay the officers, the police, for what that officer did to my son when he lied on the stand, I was going to do it. I didn't care what happened. It wasn't much of anything, assault third degree-a fight, and not too serious an injury. But I thought this was a good time to make sure that I came across with my belief that the police officer was a liar. That, your honor, is the sum and substance of why I held out against a conviction."

Well, I thought that was unusual but, you know, a juror can do whatever he wants. He can find a defendant guilty or not guilty whether the evidence points to guilt or not, whether he should be--many times, I guess, a defendant may even be found guilty when he's not guilty but that's our system and nobody has ever figured out a better one. People in America who are charged with a crime have a right to a jury trial of their peers. Not a jury made up of somebody from California or Louisiana but a jury of their peers chosen from their own community. She chose for reasons of her own, maybe right, maybe wrong, maybe good, maybe bad-- but that's the system. There's nothing we can do about it except change the system and I don't believe we want to do that. By and large, the system works, by and large it's satisfactory, and by and large I think we're going to continue with it.

Case Twenty Eight
Involuntary Servitude

This case was an odd one. A State Policeman came to my office. He was with the BCI, the Bureau of Criminal Investigation, and he said there was a doctor's wife in my community, my jurisdiction, who apparently was guilty of involuntary servitude. A fancy name for slavery, I guess.

He told me that he was asked to investigate the case because the NCAA, that is the colored organization, had contacted the Governor and told the Governor what was happening and they wanted some action taken. The Governor turned it over to me and here I am. I have to see you. I've already talked to the party against whom the complaint was filed. I said, "Well, tell me about it."

The State Policeman told me that the doctor's wife, seeking to employ permanent help for the house, a housemaid, someone who could help with the housework, saw an Ad in the local paper that was put there by some young Afro/American, black girl, from Georgia. She called the girl on the phone and made arrangements for her to come to Solvay and go to work for her. She sent her the money for the train fare and I believe she said she sent her some money to buy some food or snacks or whatever. Things worked out satisfactorily in the beginning, it seems. This young girl about 16 years of age or 17 years of age worked in the house-did the housework, did the dishes, helped with the cooking and did all the things that the doctor's wife had expected here to do and was pleased with her work.

But after about two or three weeks she began to go out evenings and wouldn't come back to the house until about 2:00 or 3:00 o'clock in the morning and it was awfully hard getting her up in the morning to do her work. She would sleep until noontime most of the time and half the time she was still half sleepy. Anyway, it wasn't working out--it wasn't satisfactory. The doctor's wife told the girl she could not do this, she could not continue. If she wanted to go out and have fun, reserve the time and do it on the week end--Saturday night. Then if she came home late Saturday night that's to be understood. But during the week and two or three times a week to be running out and coming home late would not be allowed, would not be tolerated. So, she said, I think it best if you continuously keep doing this that we discontinue our relationship and you go back to Georgia.

Well, the young girl said she was sorry for what happened and said she wasn't going to do it any more. She was going to tend to her job, do her work, go to sleep early enough at night so she could be up the next day and do her work around the house. It didn't turn out that way--for two or three nights, yes; but then she continued to go out evenings again, coming home late and doing everything that she did before. So the doctor's wife said, "That's it. I'm gonna buy you a train ticket and send you back to Georgia. I'll also give you a little money that you can use to buy some snacks or something. But you'll have to work here for another week or ten days to pay me for the train fare."

The young girl didn't like the idea, first of being sent back to Georgia where she didn't want to go back there because she was really enjoying herself here in Syracuse. But she also didn't like the idea that she'd have to work without pay and that instead of being paid, the doctor's wife would buy a train ticket to send her back to Georgia.

At any rate, she told this situation, or problem to her boy friend. He contacted the National Association of Colored People, told them the story and said, "The doctor's wife is trying to make this girl work for nothing. Work all week, ten days, and not get paid." He said, "That's like slavery." They sent the complaint to the Governor, the Governor gave it to me and here I am. I said to the trooper, "I think that's stretching things a bit. But I'll send for the doctor's wife and get her side of the story," which I did.

We waited a little while, the doctor's wife came in and we told her what was happening and that there was a serious chance that she might even be charged with a crime. Well, you can imagine how shocked she was to think that with the circumstances being what they were that she would be charged with a crime when it turns out this young girl who came here from Georgia, didn't live up to her agreement--for weeks on end didn't perform, didn't do her work. Here she was not wanting to go back to Georgia and seriously considering bringing charges against her. I said, "Well, they haven't presented any charges yet, but we've got to resolve it. So I'll tell you what, I'm going to adjourn this matter until next Monday or Tuesday, depending on how you feel about it, and we're going to have to send for this young lady and have her tell us, herself, what happened.

We did this. The young lady told me she did not want to go back to Georgia, she liked it where she is. She likes being up here in the North. She said, "There's more freedom, more fun, more things to do." She also said she was sorry things didn't work out but she said she didn't think this lady had a right to tell her, "You're going back to Georgia." She also said, "I don't think she can make me work for ten days so they could buy a ticket to send me back to Georgia, especially when I didn't want to go." I said, "Well, you're free to do as you please. You're free to stay here in Central New York. You don't have to go back to Georgia if you don't choose, you don't have to work for the doctor's wife if you don't choose and, from what I can see here, you going to have a tough time finding employment and sticking to the job because you can't have it both ways. You can't be going out nights coming home at 2:00 and 3:00 o'clock in the morning and then shirking your work, shirking your job. So I don't think there's any evidence here to prove what your boy friend said was slavery. There isn't any evidence here to indicate that you were being held involuntarily in servitude. You're free to go, you have been and you're free to do as you please. That's as far as I'm going with this case. I'm not going to allow any further action or prosecution to take place."

I turned to the doctor's wife and said, "I hope you've learned a lesson from this. Sending away to a Southern State for some colored girl to come here and work for you is not the way to go. Put an Ad in the paper. There are a lot of young people, there are a lot of older people for that matter, who'd be glad to work for you and do your housework. They wouldn't necessarily have to be living with you. They just come there in the daytime, do their work, and go home. That's the way it should be. You weren't helping her out anyway. As a matter of fact, you were only getting yourself in trouble."

So I turned to the State Policeman who was there at the session and I said, "You can report back to the Governor that I find no evidence whatsoever of involuntary servitude and that I am not going to take any action and I'm not going to permit any action to be taken in my court." The State Policeman looked at me and he said, "I totally agree, your honor, and I'm going to make it very emphatically clear to the Governor that this brainstorm was one created by this girl's boy friend because he didn't want her to go to Georgia. At any rate, I'm satisfied that you handled it properly."

Case Twenty Nine
Innocent by Reason of Insanity

I had reason to listen to the evidence in a murder case. The defendant was insane. He had been discharged from the Army because he was insane, but the institution where he had been placed let him go home on certain week ends and it was on one of these particular weekends that he got mad at his wife, got his Army rifle out, shot and killed her. I listened to all of this testimony and I decided this fellow was "wacko". This fellow has been discharged from service because he was insane. He had been sent to Canindago State Hospital for the Mentally Insane, because he was "wacko." I said it was my decision that he could not be held and charged with first degree murder. I said, "He is insane and I'm sure a jury will find that he is innocent because of insanity." So, I said, "What we can do with this man is send him back to Canindago with an order that he is not to be released ever, except on my say so. He is never to be released even temporarily, or even for a short time, or even for a weekend. He is not to be released at any time or for any reason without first consulting with me and getting my authority to do so because I still have pending here a charge against him for first degree murder."

The District Attorney who conducted the hearing didn't like my decision, which is alright, and presented all the same evidence to the Grand Jury and the Grand Jury indicted him for first degree murder. A trial was conducted in County Court. I assume the same evidence was presented. At any rate, the jury came out after all the testimony had been taken and said in essence, "We find the defendant 'not guilty' by reason of insanity." So here, after very large sums of money had been spent to try this man and after all the people involved had spent their time prosecuting this man, the decision with reference to how he was to be handled was just as I had determined it should be when I had the preliminary hearing.

Now don't get me wrong, he is not released because he's found innocent by reason of insanity. He is sent to Canidago State Hospital for the Mentally Insane to remain forever and never to be released. And also, the decision is, by the County Court --if he should ever recover from his insanity then he would have to stand trial because his innocence was determined by the fact that he was declared insane. In other words, you can't be found guilty of murder unless you know what you're doing--unless you're sane, unless you have control of your faculties. A person who's insane certainly doesn't know what he's doing, why he's doing it. He doesn't realize what the outcome of his actions will be. I mention this case because the District Attorney's Office didn't believe that I had made the right decision. And, of course, as it turned out, I did.

Case Thirty
Fuel Bill

This is one that I really wasn't very happy about. I didn't like it at all, but I had to do my duty and I did so. This was Christmas Eve Day. The Sergeant at the desk called me on the phone and said, "I have a matter here I don't know how to handle, I'd better have you come over here and decide what to do." I said, "Alright." You know that happened frequently. The police didn't know sometimes--or an actual crime they weren't sure was committed. So I went over to the police station and learned as follows.

The mother of these two kids, two daughters, I think one was twelve or so and the other was fourteen, called the police station and told them that they were all freezing to death, they didn't have any heat and the temperature in the house was about 25 or 30 degrees.

The Sergeant said, "Well, come on over to the police station, we'll call the Judge and we'll see what we can do about it." When I got there, she told me that she and her husband were separated, that he gave her a certain amount of money every week pursuant to an order of the Family Court Judge and she said that the fuel man wasn't going to deliver any more oil for their furnace because he hadn't been paid for his last delivery which was $14.15. I said to the lady, "Well, you get a certain amount of money each week from your husband?" She said, "Yes." I said, "How much?" She said, "Twenty dollars." And I said With that $20 you're supposed to buy food for the children, furnish them clothes, pay for a dentist or doctor in case they need it?" She said, "Yes." "I suppose from that money you could save some so you could pay for the heat?" She said, "Yes, I called my husband and told him I couldn't pay for the fuel and that he would have to pay so that I could get another order of fuel for the furnace." He said, "I give you enough money every week. You should budget the money I give you and make means for paying for fuel oil." She said I told him however, that last week I didn't work and my allowance from him was dependant in part upon how much money I got because I was working too. But I didn't work last week because I was sick so I didn't have the money to pay for the fuel. I said, "Okay."

I turned to the police officer and I said, "Did you check the temperature in the house?" He said, "Yes. Your honor, the temperature in that house was freezing. It was about 35 degrees. The kids were all bundled up, huddled in a corner and they were freezing." I said, "Okay." I turned to the lady and I said, "Where's you husband? Where does he work?" She said, "Well, he's at such and such an address, and he can be reached right now because I talked to him a little while ago and he told me he wasn't going to do anything about it." I said, "Okay." So I called him on the phone and I said, "Sir, we found out your two daughters were down there at the house practically freezing to death, the temperature is around 25, the police have checked it, the wife tells me you won't pay the oil man for the last delivery; therefore, they won't deliver any oil for this purpose and it's for that reason that until they get paid for the last delivery they're not going to make another delivery until they get paid for the last one. I suggest that you call the delivery man and tell them that you'll have a check ready to pay them. He said, "Whoa, whoa, hold on your honor. I'm not paying anybody for any oil. I give her money every week and expect she's supposed to save something out of that money to pay for fuel oil." I said, "Sir, please listen to me. This is Christmas Eve Day. Your kids, these are your children aren't they?" He said, "Yes." I said, "Your kids are down there freezing. I don't know what goes on between you and your wife, why the heat isn't paid for, why you don't have heat down there, but I do know that they're freezing. It's Christmas Eve Night, tomorrow is Christmas, and they need to have heat. You and your wife can figure this all out afterwards. Go to the Family Court Judge and talk to him about what happened and maybe he can make some adjustment as to what your payment should be or shouldn't be, I don't care. But for the time being, I want you to pay for that last fuel bill so they'll make the delivery and get some heat in that house for those kids." He said, "No, I'm not gonna do it and you can't make me." I said, "I can't?" He said, "No." I said, "Alright" and hung up. I said to the Sergeant, "Go down and arrest that fellow, bring him in here." He said, "What will I charge him with?" I said, "I'll figure something, but in the meantime if he asks you, tell him he's being charged with neglect of his children, they're freezing to death, they may get very sick and probably could die. So you tell him the judge wants to see him because he wants to talk to him to see what can be done to prevent the kids from getting sick."

The Sergeant went out and about half an hour or an hour later he came back with the father. If looks could kill, I'd be dead. He said, "Why am I here?" I said,

"You're here because I want you to pay for that last fuel bill so these kids can have some heat over the Holiday." He said, "I'm not gonna do it, and you can't make me." "I can't?" "No." I said to the Sergeant, "Lock him up." He said, "You can't do that." I said, "Lock him up." The Sergeant took him down the stairs. All the way down he kept saying, "You can't do this, you can't do this." I even heard the gate clang shut and he was still hollering about I couldn't lock him up. But he did holler up at one time, "I want to talk to my lawyer." I said to the Sergeant, "Let him out and let him use that phone down there. Let him talk to the lawyer." He talked to the lawyer and then the lawyer told the Sergeant, let me talk to the Judge. I told him the story and he said, "Oh, my God. He didn't tell me that the kids were down there freezing. He just told me that he gives his wife money she's supposed to use to pay for all the things they need and they didn't pay the bill for the heat and they weren't going to deliver any more oil. But he didn't tell me that the kids were freezing." I said, "No, he didn't." I said, "As a matter of fact that's the only reason why I locked him up." He said, "What are you going to charge him with, Judge?" I said, "I'm going to charge him with neglect of his children." "Oh, I see. Well, let me talk to him." So he put the father back on the phone again and he was telling his lawyer why he wasn't going to pay for it. So I said, "Okay, bring him up here." So I brought him up to the bench and I said, "John, (name fictitious) let me tell you something, this is Christmas Eve Day, tomorrow is Christmas. I'm going to call the fuel company to tell them to deliver another delivery to your house. I'm going to tell them to stop here and pick up a check for $14.150 which either you or I are going to pay. If I pay it, you go downstairs, get locked up again and I won't be seeing you until the day after Christmas. You won't be out on bail, you won't be able to get your lawyer because he won't be available and you're going to spend Christmas Eve and Christmas Day in jail if I have to pay for that fuel bill." "Oh", he said "That's the way it is huh?" I said, "Yep, if you want to stay out of jail and don't want to go down the stairs in that cell again, you'd better make out a check so when the oil man comes here we can give it to him. If you don't, I will." Well he thought better of it and thought it would be best if he paid that fuel bill because I guess he didn't like the idea of going downstairs and being locked up in the jail cell for Christmas Eve and Christmas Day.

But I tell that story because I think it's important for people to know that the kids cannot, should not, ever be punished because the two parents cannot get along. And as long as I was judge I never allowed it to happen because I had a real weapon and that weapon was "Neglect of Children" and I was going to use it and if the culprits did not do what they were supposed to, to take care of their own children, they would be going to jail. Let me tell you, that's the kind of sentence I really liked to exact.

Case Thirty One
Speed Trap

The next case involves a traffic violation. It's kind of an odd one at that because what had happened was that the police department had bought a traffic trap, that's what I called it.

The police thought it would be a nice gadget to use to try pick up speeders but most of all it was very useful especially when you were determining whether the defendant was speeding or not because once they went over that line, I guess there were two lines, and that the distance between the two lines would indicate the speed they were traveling and so they had come evidence to back them up whenever they issued a ticket.

I thought this was a good item and I thought it would help the police. I, as I said, really thought it was a good gimmick because it would help the police control the speeding in the village. The problem was, they laid the speed line just inside the village limits and people coming down, before they approached the village limits would be allowed to go 40 miles per hour, then there would be a sign saying, "You are entering the Village of Solvay, Speed Limit 25", but they would put the speed trap as I call it right there just inside the village line. So you can imagine somebody driving along at 40 miles an hour suddenly seeing a sign that says, "You're are entering the Village of Solvay, Speed Limit 25," how the devil are you going to get from 40 miles an hour right down to 25 in a matter of about 15 or 20 feet.

Well, that's what happened. About three or four speeders were brought before me the next morning after they had installed this so-called speed trap. They all gave me the same story. It appears that they said were going along the highway at 40 miles an hour and suddenly there appears this sign that says, "You are entering the Village of Solvay," and just as they hit the Village of Solvay Line, the speed limit dropped to 25. They said they couldn't do so. They slammed on the brakes, tried to reduce their speed but couldn't do it in that short a period of time.

So I adjourned the cases and told them all to appear before me two days later in the morning at about 9:30 and I was going to find out what had happened. I did.

I asked the Chief of Police what happened and he told me I should talk to the Lieutenant. I had the Lieutenant come in to see me and I said, "These drivers tell me that the speed limit of 25 miles an hour in Solvay, and prior to reaching this point they were allowed to go 40 and then just as they hit the Village line here was this line across the highway which would pick up and was used to determine the speed." I said, "I kind of agree that this is not really what the purpose of those speed gadgets are. I think that it's unfair and I'm not going to hold these men guilty of speeding in the Village because they hadn't gone ten feet in the Village before they were picked up for speeding. I think you should arrange to have your men set that speed trap maybe about 50 or 100 yards from the Village line and then if they're going over the 25 miles an hour speed limit, it would be appropriate to give them a ticket for speeding." He acknowledged what I said, but didn't seem to be too happy about the fact that I was going to dismiss these cases against the three speeders they had picked up. But I figured that on reflection later on he would find out for himself that this was unfair.

You don't set up the line just inside your Village or City Limits and expect a person going 40 miles an hour to slow down to 25 miles an hour within a matter of ten yards from the line. "As a matter of fact," I said "you wouldn't pick up a speeder for going over 25 miles an hour if you didn't have that trap. If they're going 40 miles an hour before they get to the Village Limits, slow down to maybe 30 then later on to 25, you'd be satisfied that they're abiding by the speed limit laws. I'm sorry, but that's how I feel. I feel it's unfair and I don't think that's the purpose for which we have this new gimmick to pick up speeders. I think this is a mechanism by which you can determine how fast people are going in the Village, in the streets and so forth, but certainly not for the purpose of arresting people and bringing them before me just so we can catch so many speeders. I hope you don't think that's what we're going to do here to pay for this new piece of machinery that we got to catch speeders.

Case Thirty Two
Defendant Represents Self

As I said before, I had one case that appeared before me in the Small Claims Court that I thought was quite amusing and, therefore, I'm gonna report it It seems that this is a case in which the plaintiff sued the defendant on a promissory note for $250. The case was set on my court and was set for trial in what we call the "Small Claims" Court.

I wondered very much why this had to go to trial because if there was a promissory note involved, if it could be shown that there was fraud or coercion or anything of that kind, maybe that would be the defense that the defendant would show in the course of the trial. But you know, as I told you earlier, in Small Claims Court trials there are no attorneys present--only the parties involved and the judge. There is no jury. No jury trial is allowed. It's just a matter of sort of an informal court procedure. The judge is the sole determiner of what the outcome should be.

Well, in this case I questioned whether or not it should be even tried but it so happened that the parties came in and the plaintiff presented his evidence which was the promissory note which had been signed by the defendant and he said, "Your honor this is all I got," he said "I gave the man the money which was $250 and he signed the note and when it came due three months later and I asked for the money, he wouldn't pay it. I was kind of shocked in a way because he's not a total stranger to me. He's sort of a acquaintance, or a friend you might say, and I was surprised he didn't want to pay me back the $250 I loaned him. Well, anyway, that's my case."

I turned to the defendant and said, "Well, we are at trial here so go ahead and let's proceed." He said, "I want to question him, if you please, your honor, I want to question the plaintiff." I said, "Sure that's your privilege." He asked the plaintiff, "Was this note signed by me?" The plaintiff said, "Yes." "That's good." He said, "Did you exercise coercion of any kind forcing me to sign this?" He said, "No." "That's good." He said, "Did you give me the money, the $250, at the time I signed the note?" "Yes, you're the one that I gave the money." "That's good." He said, "Do you think there was any fraud committed here like somebody committing some fraud of some kind?" The plaintiff said, "No. There's no fraud. It's just a simple case of my loaning you the money, you signing this note payable in 90 days. That's about it." So he said, "That's all, I have nothing further to ask this plaintiff. My case rests."

I said, "I still fail to see why this had to come to trial You signed a note. You better than anybody else know whether there was any fraud or coercion. You better than anybody else know whether there was any consideration-you got the $250. That was certainly consideration for the signing of the note. Why did you let it come to trial?" "Well", he said "Your Honor, all my life I had one real desire and that was to be a lawyer. Things didn't work out that way so I never got to be a lawyer but I knew that this time, under these circumstances, I had one chance to be my own lawyer. I didn't want to lose the opportunity so I have come to court for no reason at all except to be and act like a lawyer. That's about it, your honor." I said, "Yes, the only thing is, my friend, you're going to have to pay the $250 which I guess you understand anyway but you're going to have to pay the costs. The plaintiff here had to have papers served on you and those papers, the summons and complaint and court fees. You have to pay an additional $65. I suppose that's not bad tuition for being able to practice law. Well, good luck to both of you. I'm glad that you got the experience of being a lawyer. Of course you got the money back that you loaned. Okay, next case."

Case Thirty Three
Neighbor Plucks Fruit

The sergeant at the desk didn't know what to do with this next case because it was sort of unusual-not in the general run-of-the-mill type of cases. It seems that this lady came over to the court house and wanted to file a complaint against her neighbor. It seems that, she said, the neighbor was in violation of her rights. In other words, the neighbor had plucked the cherries off the cherry tree, the limbs, which extended over the border line into his land. He just reached up plucked the cherries, took them in and consumed them.

She thought he ought to pay for those cherries because they were cherries that were on her tree. The tree was in her yard and he had no right to go picking cherries off the tree and not paying for them. So, of course, the sergeant didn't think that was quite a theft case in itself. That's why he sent for me. I went over and heard the same story. I said, "Ma 'am, were these limbs from which he plucked those cherries over his land; did they extend from your tree over past the line between your two properties?" "Yes", she said "They reached over there." I said, "Well, Ma 'am, the owner of that property had one of two options. He could either pluck the fruit off the tree, if it was a fruit tree, on any branches that extended over his land because he owns everything from his line straight up to space and those tree limbs naturally would be over his property; so if they're on his property he has a right to pluck the fruit. The other alternative, or other option he has, would be to cut those limbs at the point where they extend beyond your property into his property. Now that's the law. Of course, when he cuts those limbs, if he does, he has to make sure that he does so in such a fashion that he doesn't cause the tree to die. In other words, he has to doctor up those various areas where he sawed off the limbs.

"It appears that this party, your next door neighbor, chose to let the limbs grow over his land and as a result he decided a good idea was to harvest some cherries from a cherry tree and he didn't have to bother trimming, taking care of, fertilizing and all that. Now that's the sum and substance of it, Ma'am, you don't have any

223

complaint. You have no right to sue him and there is nothing here for which you can get any relief. You had better make sure when he decides, if he should decide, to cut the limbs off the tree that he cuts them at a point where they extend beyond his own line. That's about it. I can't help you, Ma 'am, because that's the law."

THE END

That's about the end of the cases which I thought might be of some interest either because they were interesting or humorous and now I've come to the end of the book but before I close, before I finish, I do want to add one admonishment which I think would be very helpful to people who read this book and that is if on any occasion you should happen to come before a judge, I want you to know that the President of the United States cannot send you to jail, the Governor of the State cannot send you to jail, the mayor of a city cannot send you to jail. There is only one person in our system of Government that can send you to jail and that's the judge. My warning to you is as follows: If it should happen that you have to appear before a judge, please be very respectful, be very courteous, kill him with kindness, because remember he's the only one that can send you to jail and remember also that if you're very nice to him, very kind, very respectful, it makes it awfully hard for a judge to send you to jail. One the other hand, if you're obnoxious, if you take out your anger on the judge that you have for the policeman who gave you the ticket, or if you in any way act disrespectful or you are discourteous, don't make it easy for the judge to send you to jail. That's my advice to you and I hope you follow it.

I'm not sure, but I think all books end up with two words--"The End", and that's what I have here for my book.